MYP *by Conc*

3

English

Ana de Castro
Zara Kaiserimam

Series editor: Paul Morris

A note about spelling: We have followed IB house style for spelling of certain words, using –ize rather than –ise; and vice versa.

There is a widespread belief that -ize is American English and that British English should use the –ise forms, but for certain verbs/words both endings are correct in British English. The important thing to remember is to be consistent in a piece of writing.

You can find out more information here: http://blog.oxforddictionaries.com/2011/03/ize-or-ise/

A note about command terms: There are five specific command terms for language acquisition – analyse, evaluate, identify, interpret and synthesize. We have emboldened these five command terms in the book, alongside the wider MYP command terms, so that you familiarise yourself with these terms.

Authors' dedication

Ana de Castro – For Neli, who loves books, and for Jorge, who learnt to love them

Zara Kaiserimam – For my favourites, Isa and Haniah

Although every effort has been made to ensure that website addresses are correct at time of going to press, Hodder Education cannot be held responsible for the content of any website mentioned in this book. It is sometimes possible to find a relocated web page by typing in the address of the home page for a website in the URL window of your browser.

Hachette Livre UK's policy is to use papers that are natural, renewable and recyclable products and made from wood grown in sustainable forests. The logging and manufacturing processes are expected to conform to the environmental regulations of the country of origin.

Orders: please contact Bookpoint Ltd, 130 Milton Park, Abingdon, Oxon OX14 4SB. Telephone: (44) 01235 827720. Fax: (44) 01235 400454. Lines are open from 9.00–5.00, Monday to Saturday, with a 24 hour message answering service. You can also order through our website www.hoddereducation.com

© Ana de Castro and Zara Kaiserimam 2017
Published by Hodder Education
An Hachette UK Company
Carmelite House, 50 Victoria Embankment, London EC4Y 0DZ

Impression number   5 4 3 2 1
Year   2020 2019 2018 2017

Cover photo © Arenaphotouk/123RF.com
Illustrations by DC Graphic Design Limited
Typeset in Frutiger LT Std 45 Light 11/15pt by DC Graphic Design Limited, Hextable, Kent
Printed in Slovenia

A catalogue record for this title is available from the British Library

ISBN 9781471880674

Contents

1 Am I ready for the real world? 2

2 What's that you said? 20

3 How can we overcome difficult challenges? 40

4 Can we travel through writing? 60

5 Is tradition worth preserving? 90

6 How do you see the world? 124

Glossary 154

Acknowledgements 155

How to use this book

Welcome to Hodder Education's *MYP by Concept* Series! Each chapter is designed to lead you through an *inquiry* into the concepts of Language acquisition, and how they interact in real-life global contexts.

The *Statement of Inquiry* provides the framework for this inquiry, and the *Inquiry questions* then lead us through the exploration as they are developed through each chapter.

KEY WORDS

Key words are included to give you access to vocabulary for the topic. **Glossary terms** are highlighted and, where applicable, **search terms** are given to encourage independent learning and research skills.

As you explore, activities suggest ways to learn through *action*.

■ ATL

Activities are designed to develop your *Approaches to Learning* (ATL) skills.

◆ Assessment opportunities in this chapter:

Some activities are *formative* as they allow you to practise certain parts of the MYP Language acquisition *Assessment Objectives*. Other activities can be used by you or your teachers to assess your achievement *summatively* against all parts of an assessment objective.

Each chapter is framed with a *Key concept*, *Related concept* and set in a *Global context*.

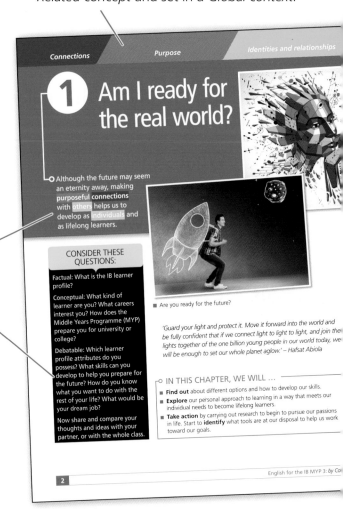

| Connections | Purpose | Identities and relationships |

1 Am I ready for the real world?

Although the future may seem an eternity away, making **purposeful** **connections** with **others** helps us to develop as **individuals** and as lifelong learners.

CONSIDER THESE QUESTIONS:

Factual: What is the IB learner profile?

Conceptual: What kind of learner are you? What careers interest you? How does the Middle Years Programme (MYP) prepare you for university or college?

Debatable: Which learner profile attributes do you possess? What skills can you develop to help you prepare for the future? How do you know what you want to do with the rest of your life? What would be your dream job?

Now share and compare your thoughts and ideas with your partner, or with the whole class.

■ Are you ready for the future?

'Guard your light and protect it. Move it forward into the world and be fully confident that if we connect light to light to light, and join the lights together of the one billion young people in our world today, we will be enough to set our whole planet aglow.' – Hafsat Abiola

○ IN THIS CHAPTER, WE WILL ...

■ **Find out** about different options and how to develop our skills.
■ **Explore** our personal approach to learning in a way that meets our individual needs to become lifelong learners.
■ **Take action** by carrying out research to begin to pursue our passions in life. Start to **identify** what tools are at our disposal to help us work toward our goals.

Key *Approaches to Learning* skills for MYP Language acquisition are highlighted whenever we encounter them.

Hint

In some of the activities, we provide hints to help you work on the assignment. This also introduces you to the new Hint feature in the on-screen assessment.

❶

Definitions are included for important terms and information boxes are included to give background information, more detail and explanation.

You are prompted to consider your conceptual understanding in a variety of activities throughout each chapter.

We have incorporated Visible Thinking – ideas, framework, protocol and thinking routines – from Project Zero at the Harvard Graduate School of Education into many of our activities.

▼ Links to:

Like any other subject, Language acquisition is just one part of our bigger picture of the world. Links to other subjects are discussed.

● We will reflect on this learner profile attribute …

- Each chapter has an *IB learner profile* attribute as its theme, and you are encouraged to reflect on these too.

Finally, at the end of the chapter you are asked to reflect back on what you have learnt with our *Reflection table*, maybe to think of new questions brought to light by your learning.

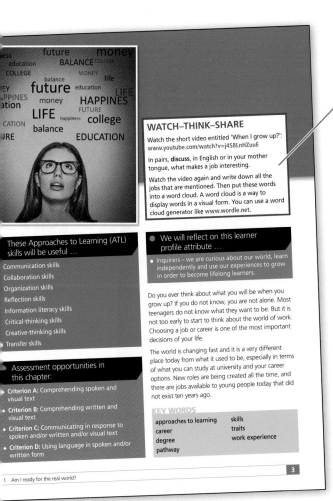

WATCH–THINK–SHARE

Watch the short video entitled 'When I grow up?':
www.youtube.com/watch?v=j4S8LnHZuuE

In pairs, **discuss**, in English or in your mother tongue, what makes a job interesting.

Watch the video again and write down all the jobs that are mentioned. Then put these words into a word cloud. A word cloud is a way to display words in a visual form. You can use a word cloud generator like www.wordle.net.

These Approaches to Learning (ATL) skills will be useful …

Communication skills
Collaboration skills
Organization skills
Reflection skills
Information literacy skills
Critical-thinking skills
Creative-thinking skills
▶ Transfer skills

Assessment opportunities in this chapter:

◆ **Criterion A:** Comprehending spoken and visual text
◆ **Criterion B:** Comprehending written and visual text
◆ **Criterion C:** Communicating in response to spoken and/or written and/or visual text
◆ **Criterion D:** Using language in spoken and/or written form

● We will reflect on this learner profile attribute …

- Inquirers – we are curious about our world, learn independently and use our experiences to grow in order to become lifelong learners.

Do you ever think about what you will be when you grow up? If you do not know, you are not alone. Most teenagers do not know what they want to be. But it is not too early to start to think about the world of work. Choosing a job or career is one of the most important decisions of your life.

The world is changing fast and it is a very different place today from what it used to be, especially in terms of what you can study at university and your career options. New roles are being created all the time, and there are jobs available to young people today that did not exist ten years ago.

KEY WORDS

approaches to learning	skills
career	traits
degree	work experience
pathway	

1 Am I ready for the real world?

3

EXTENSION

Extension activities allow you to explore a topic further.

! Take action

! While the book provides opportunities for action and plenty of content to enrich the conceptual relationships, you must be an active part of this process. Guidance is given to help you with your own research, including how to carry out research, guidance on forming your own research question, as well as linking and developing your study of Language acquisition to the global issues in our twenty-first-century world.

Use this table to reflect on your own learning in this chapter					
Questions we asked	Answers we found	Any further questions now?			
Factual					
Conceptual					
Debatable					
Approaches to learning you used in this chapter	Description – what new skills did you learn?	How well did you master the skills?			
		Novice	Learner	Practitioner	Expert
Learner profile attribute(s)	Reflect on the importance of the attribute for your learning in this chapter.				

1 Am I ready for the real world?

Although the future may seem an eternity away, making **purposeful connections** with **others** helps us to develop as **individuals** and as lifelong learners.

CONSIDER THESE QUESTIONS:

Factual: What is the IB learner profile?

Conceptual: What kind of learner are you? What careers interest you? How does the Middle Years Programme (MYP) prepare you for university or college?

Debatable: Which learner profile attributes do you possess? What skills can you develop to help you prepare for the future? How do you know what you want to do with the rest of your life? What would be your dream job?

Now **share and compare** your thoughts and ideas with your partner, or with the whole class.

■ Are you ready for the future?

'Guard your light and protect it. Move it forward into the world and be fully confident that if we connect light to light to light, and join the lights together of the one billion young people in our world today, we will be enough to set our whole planet aglow.' – Hafsat Abiola

IN THIS CHAPTER, WE WILL …

■ **Find out** about different options and how to develop our skills.

■ **Explore** our personal approach to learning in a way that meets our individual needs to become lifelong learners.

■ **Take action** by carrying out research to begin to pursue our passions in life. Start to **identify** what tools are at our disposal to help us work toward our goals.

WATCH–THINK–SHARE

Watch the short video entitled 'When I grow up?': www.youtube.com/watch?v=j4S8LnHZuuE

In pairs, **discuss**, in English or in your mother tongue, what makes a job interesting.

Watch the video again and write down all the jobs that are mentioned. Then put these words into a word cloud. A word cloud is a way to display words in a visual form. You can use a word cloud generator like www.wordle.net.

■ These Approaches to Learning (ATL) skills will be useful …

- ■ Communication skills
- ■ Collaboration skills
- ■ Organization skills
- ■ Reflection skills
- ■ Information literacy skills
- ■ Critical-thinking skills
- ■ Creative-thinking skills
- ■ Transfer skills

◆ Assessment opportunities in this chapter:

- ◆ **Criterion A:** Comprehending spoken and visual text
- ◆ **Criterion B:** Comprehending written and visual text
- ◆ **Criterion C:** Communicating in response to spoken and/or written and/or visual text
- ◆ **Criterion D:** Using language in spoken and/or written form

● We will reflect on this learner profile attribute …

- ● Inquirers – we are curious about our world, learn independently and use our experiences to grow in order to become lifelong learners.

Do you ever think about what you will be when you grow up? If you do not know, you are not alone. Most teenagers do not know what they want to be. But it is not too early to start to think about the world of work. Choosing a job or career is one of the most important decisions of your life.

The world is changing fast and it is a very different place today from what it used to be, especially in terms of what you can study at university and your career options. New roles are being created all the time, and there are jobs available to young people today that did not exist ten years ago.

KEY WORDS

approaches to learning	skills
career	traits
degree	work experience
pathway	

What is the IB learner profile?

- At the heart of the IB is the 'learner profile' – this is the IB mission statement translated into a set of learning outcomes for the twenty-first century

WHICH LEARNER PROFILE ATTRIBUTES DO YOU POSSESS?

How do the International Baccalaureate Programmes prepare you for university or college? Well, you might find it interesting to know that there is research that looks at how well students who have done these programmes do not only at Diploma level but also at university and college. The results compare students from the MYP to students who have completed other programmes, and they are very positive. The MYP approach encourages you to think for yourself and to see the difference between classroom information and the world today.

There are schools that offer other programmes as well as IB courses. Sometimes there is competition about which programme is the best! Everyone believes that their programme is the best option. But what exactly makes the MYP special? It is true to say that one of the main differences is that the MYP not only encourages you to be an independent inquirer but also allows you to explore connections between all the subjects, and you get to complete a personal project which involves lots of research.

THINK–PAIR–SHARE

■ ATL

- Creative-thinking skills: Practise visible thinking strategies and techniques

Individually, **design** a logo (a symbol) using your name. Use your imagination – you can design by hand or by computer, you can incorporate motion or animation. Go wherever your creativity leads you! There is only one condition: your logo must reflect who you are.

In pairs, **discuss** how you came up with the design and why you chose to make it this way. You can **explain** your design in your mother tongue.

◆ Assessment opportunities

- ◆ This activity can be assessed using Criterion D: Using language in spoken and/or written form.

ACTIVITY: Unique and shared

■ ATL

- Collaboration skills: Exercise leadership and take on a variety of roles within groups

Unique and shared is a game to find out what we have in common with our peers, in other words, our similarities, but also to find out what our own strengths are.

First, in groups of four or five, take a sheet of paper and decide who will take notes for your group.

In your group, **create** a list of the *shared* traits and qualities that the members of the group have. For example, 'We all have siblings'. Try not to write things that are too obvious. The idea is to try and and find strengths and characteristics that are not superficial. You have 5 minutes to do this.

ACTIVITY: The magic lamp

■ ATL

- Collaboration skills: Negotiate effectively; Build consensus

In pairs or groups of three, imagine that you have just found a lamp. You rub it and are surprised when a genie appears! The genie of the lamp tells you that you can have three wishes related to your school life. In your groups, agree on the three wishes you want to present to the genie. On a large piece of paper, write down your wish list. **Present** your wish list to the rest of the class and say why you want the genie to grant these wishes.

◆ Assessment opportunities

- This activity can be assessed using Criterion D: Using language in spoken and/or written form.

Now, **select** a member of the group to read your list to the rest of the class.

For the second part of the game, the *unique* part, work in new groups of four or five with different people. **Select** someone in the group to be the notetaker. Take another sheet of paper and write down unique characteristics for each member of the group. You must try to find at least two unique qualities for each person. Remember to try and choose things that are not superficial. You have another 5 minutes to complete this task. Nominate someone in the group to read a quality, one at a time, to the class. See if your classmates can guess whose quality it is.

◆ Assessment opportunities

- This activity can be assessed using Criterion D: Using language in spoken and/or written form.

ACTIVITY: How does the MYP compare?

■ ATL

- Information literacy skills: Access information to be informed and inform others
- Creative-thinking skills: Use brainstorming and visual diagrams to generate new ideas and inquiries

In pairs, go to your school website and find out basic information about the MYP programme. Now, carry out some research about a different study programme from your country.

Complete a Venn diagram with the information you have found and **present** it to your class.

A Venn diagram is a useful tool to **compare and contrast** information.

Visit this website and copy the template: **https://eslwriteaway.files.wordpress.com/2014/10/venn-diagram.jpg**

◆ Assessment opportunities

- This activity can be assessed using Criterion C: Communicating in response to spoken and/or written and/or visual text and Criterion D: Using language in spoken and/or written form.

ACTIVITY: Word cloud

■ ATL

■ Organization skills: Use appropriate strategies for organizing complex information

discovery dream job choices preferences lifelong pathway community university passion scholarship career planning volunteering college skills approaches to learning courses identity traits degree work experience gap year

In pairs, **select** words from the word cloud above and write your own **sentences**.

Use an online dictionary to check the meaning of any words that are not familiar to you.

Now **create** your own word cloud of important words to study related to the MYP, going to university or college, and careers.

◆ Assessment opportunities

◆ This activity can be assessed using Criterion D: Using language in spoken and/or written form.

ACTIVITY: Do you know the IB learner profile attributes?

■ ATL

■ Reflection skills: Consider ATL skills development
■ Transfer skills: Change the context of an inquiry to gain different perspectives
■ Communication skills: Write for different purposes

Task 1

Think of all the IB learner profile attributes. **List** them in reverse alphabetical order.

Task 2

In pairs, use an internet search engine to find descriptions of the IB learner profile attributes in your mother tongue.

Use your own words to **summarize** each of the learner profile attributes. For example: 'Caring – I help others and I am nice.'

Task 3

Individually, look at the attributes again and **identify** at least two that you feel are your strongest.

Write sentences with the attributes you have selected.

Start your sentences with 'I am balanced when I …'.

Now think about the attributes that are not your strongest. In pairs, share your answers. What can you do to develop these skills?

Task 4

In pairs, look at the images below and **identify** the different professions. **Select** three learner profile attributes that someone who does each job would need in order to be successful.

What skills can you develop to help you prepare for the future?

WHAT KIND OF LEARNER ARE YOU?

■ Approaches to Learning skills are a set of abilities that you need to develop in order to succeed in our information age

Through Approaches to Learning (ATL) in the IB programmes, you can develop skills that are useful across the curriculum and help you 'learn how to learn'. ATL skills can be learnt and taught, improved with practice and developed over time. They provide a strong foundation for learning independently and with others. ATL skills help you prepare for, and demonstrate your learning through, the various tasks and assessments that you complete.

ATL skills provide a common language that you can use to reflect on your process of learning. Understanding and using the ATL skills will help you in school, in your personal life and in any jobs you have in the future.

THINK–PAIR–SHARE

■ **ATL**

■ Reflection skills: Consider personal learning strategies

Individually, think about the following questions:
- **How do I learn best?**
- **How do I know?**
- **How do I communicate my understanding?**

In pairs, **discuss** your answers to the questions.

Share your thoughts with the rest of the class.

◆ Assessment opportunities

◆ This activity can be assessed using Criterion D: Using language in spoken and/or written form.

ACTIVITY: Test your awareness: Do the test

Task 1

Visit this website to test your awareness and do the test: www.youtube.com/watch?feature=player_embedded&v=Ahg6qcgoay4

In pairs, answer the following questions:
- **What did you see?**
- **Did you have different answers?**
- **What type of text is this?**
- **Identify** who made the clip.
- **Who is the audience?**
- **Did you see the moonwalking bear?**
- **Why do we see things differently?**

Task 2

Listen to the TedTalk 'Life lessons through tinkering' by Gever Tulley: www.ted.com/talks/gever_tulley_s_tinkering_school_in_action?language=en

Consider the following questions:
- **What is the purpose of the video?**
- **Use an online dictionary to find a synonym for the word 'tinkering'.**
- **Identify** the learner profile attributes that you see.
- **Select** a colour that best represents the video or the ideas presented.

Task 3

Visit this website and write down key words for Approaches to Learning (ATL): www.youtube.com/watch?v=XtsXBy1C26o

In pairs, use your key words to **create** a word cloud. You can use a word cloud generator like www.wordle.net.

Now, listen to Gever Tulley's TedTalk again and **select** the ATL skills that children can develop at the Tinkering School. Use the table opposite to help you **identify** the ATL skills.

Communication skills	How can I communicate through working with others?
	How do I use language to communicate?
	What communication tools do I use?
	Which ways of communicating do I need to improve on?
	How can I better communicate my understanding?
Collaboration skills	How can I work with others?
	How can they work with me?
	What successes have I had when I have worked with others?
Organization skills	How do I manage my time effectively?
	What organizational tools do I have?
	What aspects of my organization do I need to develop?
	How can I best organize myself?
Affective skills	How can I manage my state of mind?
	How can I manage how I feel?
Reflection skills	How do I reflect on my learning?
Research skills	How do I find information?
	How do I use different resources and information?
	How do I know if the information is reliable?
Thinking skills	How do I think?
	How am I creative?
	What tools can help me think in different ways?
Transfer skills	How do I transfer skills and knowledge across different subjects?
	How do I demonstrate what I know in different areas?

ACTIVITY: Teenage schoolboy cracks Isaac Newton's 300-year-old maths problem

■ ATL

■ Communication skills: Read critically and for comprehension; Write for different purposes

Task 1

Read the text on the opposite page and then answer the following questions:

1 **Identify** the type of text it is.
2 **Identify** a word that means 'discovery'.
3 Where does Ray come from?
4 What can Ray's solution do?
5 **Identify** a word that means 'inexperience'.
6 What has Ray loved to do from a very young age?
7 What does Ray say he is not good at?
8 **Identify** a word that means 'influenced'.
9 What does Ray want to study at university?
10 What does Ray's father do?
11 Which IB learner profile attribute(s) would you choose for Ray? Why?
12 Which ATL skills does Ray use?

Task 2

Ray is an extraordinary teenager. In pairs, find an example of someone extraordinary of any age in your school or community.

Make a list of questions to ask this person and then interview them. Use the answers to your interview questions to write sentences telling this person's story.

◆ Assessment opportunities

◆ This activity can be assessed using Criterion C: Communicating in response to spoken and/or written and/or visual text and Criterion D: Using language in spoken and/or written form.

ⓘ Did you know that International Youth Day is celebrated on 12 August? Visit this website and find out how you can participate in International Youth Day: **www.un.org/en/events/youthday/**

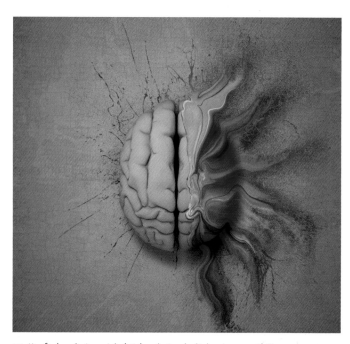

■ 'Left-brain' vs 'right-brain' – is it just a myth?

▼ Links to: Sciences

Have you wondered how the brain works? Are you a left-brain or right-brain thinker? You might have heard people say that they are good at problem-solving or better at languages. Is there a connection to how their brain works? Visit this website to find out more: **www.verywell.com/left-brain-vs-right-brain-2795005**

In pairs, carry out some research using a search engine to find out more about the **left-brain–right-brain theory**. Make notes and keep a record of the resources you have used.

What is your point of view?

Make a PowerPoint presentation and **present** this to your classmates.

Are you left-brained or right-brained?

Let's find out. Visit this website and take the test: **www.angelfire.com/wi/2brains/test.html**

Teenage schoolboy cracks Isaac Newton's 300-year-old maths problem

A 16-year-old schoolboy has solved a mathematical problem which has puzzled mathematicians for centuries, a newspaper report said. The boy put the historical breakthrough down to 'schoolboy naivety.'

Shouryya Ray, who moved to Germany from India with his family at the age of 12, has amazed scientists and mathematicians by solving two fundamental particle dynamics problems posed by Sir Isaac Newton over 350 years ago, *Die Welt* newspaper reported on Monday.

Ray's solutions make it possible to now calculate not only the flight path of a ball, but also predict how it will hit and bounce off a wall. Previously it had only been possible to estimate this using a computer, wrote the paper.

Ray first came across the old problem when his secondary school, which specializes in science, set all their year-11 pupils a research project.

On a visit to the Technical University in Dresden pupils received raw data to evaluate a direct numerical simulation – which can be used to describe the trajectory of a ball when it is thrown.

When he realised the current method could not get an exact result, Ray decided to have a go at solving it. He puts the whole thing down to 'schoolboy naivety' – he just refused to accept there was no answer to the problem.

'I asked myself: why can't it work?' he told the paper.

Ray has been fascinated by what he calls the 'essential beauty' of maths since an early age, according to the report. The boy was inspired by his engineer father who began setting him arithmetic problems at the age of six.

He recently won a youth science competition at the state level in Saxony and won second place in the Maths and IT section at the national final.

Originally from Calcutta, Ray couldn't speak a word of German when he came to Dresden four years ago – but now he is fluent. Since then, he was moved up two classes in school and is currently sitting his Abitur exams two years early.

But Ray doesn't think he's a genius, and told the paper he has weak points as a mathematician, as well as in sports and social sciences.

Ray, whose recent breakthrough may have earned him a **paragraph** in the schoolbooks of the future, is currently deciding whether to study maths or physics at university.

From www.thelocal.de

So far in this chapter we have looked at how your experiences at school can provide you with skills that will be useful later on in life. We have carefully considered the IB learner profile and Approaches to Learning skills, and the role they play in making us well-rounded members of the community. In addition, we have discovered that we all learn in different ways and that some learning approaches work better for us than others.

What careers interest you?

DO YOU KNOW ANYONE IN THAT PROFESSION?

■ As our gadgets get smaller, construction and repair of electronics will require the services of nanotechnologists

■ It is estimated that about 65 per cent of students today will be doing jobs that don't yet exist

ACTIVITY: Who can help me with my career plan?

■ **ATL**

■ Communication skills: Write for different purposes

Identifying people who can support you to develop your career plan and help you **evaluate** your choices is an important step in this process. Your supporters are those people who know you best and who can help you **identify** your interests, skills and abilities in order to find the best possible pathway to what you decide to do when you finish school.

Here are some examples of people who can help you think about your options:
- **Family**
- **Friends and family friends**
- **Current and former teachers**

Task 1

Make a list of people who support you and how you know them.

Interview them about their jobs and find out what they did in preparation for the jobs they are doing.

Task 2

Arrange to spend a day with one of these people at their place of work to learn about the working world. Keep a record of your experience. If you can, take a photo of yourself at 'work' and bring it to school to share with your class.

'The future cannot be predicted, but futures can be invented.' – Dennis Gabor, Hungarian–British electrical engineer and physicist

Use these prompts to write your reflection:

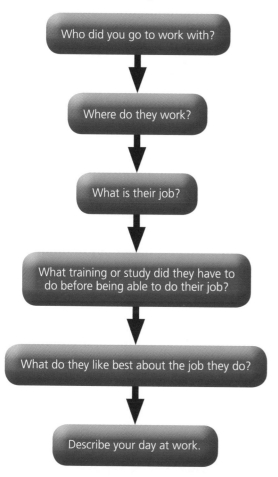

Who did you go to work with?

Where do they work?

What is their job?

What training or study did they have to do before being able to do their job?

What do they like best about the job they do?

Describe your day at work.

ACTIVITY: What do we call a person who ...?

■ ATL

■ Creative-thinking skills: Create original works and ideas; Use existing works and ideas in new ways

Task 1

In pairs, take turns to guess the job title of the person who does each of the following:

1 **Puts out fires**
2 **Fixes people's teeth**
3 **Flies an aircraft**
4 **Takes photographs**
5 **Experiments to find out new things**
6 **Makes and sells medicine**
7 **Repairs car engines**
8 **Operates on sick people**
9 **Writes newspaper articles**
10 **Sends offenders to jail**

Task 2

Now it's your turn. Make a new list of jobs and **create** your own clues. In pairs, take turns to guess what each job is.

Different ways of writing

There are four main kinds of writing that we can do. We can:

• describe what someone or something is like
• tell a story
• explain things
• argue.

To talk about what someone does and what it is like, we need to write a description. This means giving more information.

To describe a person, place or event we use **adjectives**. Adjectives are describing words that make your sentences interesting.

For example: My father works in a *busy* hospital. He is a doctor. It is a very *interesting* job.

Make a list of adjectives that you can use to describe your day at work.

ACTIVITY: Find inspiration

Task 1

- Ade Adepitan uses a wheelchair as a result of contracting polio as a child, which led to the loss of the use of his left leg

Ade Adepitan is a Paralympian. Watch this video and listen carefully to what Ade says about goals: www.bbc.co.uk/education/clips/zgn6n39

As you watch, answer the following questions:
- **Where is Ade from?**
- **What does Ade do?**
- **When did Ade's dream start?**
- **Evaluate** the purpose of the text.

- Who is the target audience for this programme? **Justify** your answer by stating which features or aspects of the programme are particularly suited to this audience.
- **Identify** how long it took Ade to reach his dream.
- Who inspired Ade?
- Do you like this video? Why? Why not?
- According to Ade, what is more important than individual success?
- Basing your answer on the final part of the video (4.09 onwards), what does Ade say anyone can achieve? **Explain** your answer by referring to information in the video.

Task 2

In pairs, read the following paragraph about 'My favourite person' and correct the mistakes:

My favourite person is My dad! He is a working very hard man, He is busy in his job, everyday 8'o clock A.m, goes out and come home, 9' o clock pm. But if he has time he plays with me and if he finish the job early, he will buy some chocolate for me and help me with my homework. He work in a big compeny and i do not now what he does but soemtimes he has to do more work when he is home. He just eat dinner, Shower, then keep doing the work. At the week end we sometimes play footbol and he is very good! My dad is funy and and very inteligent.

Now, it's your turn!

Write a 100–150-word paragraph about 'My favourite person'.

ACTIVITY: Going to college

Task 1

In groups of three or four, make a list of eight to ten universities or colleges in your country. Carry out some research to find out which websites have information about universities and colleges in your country or just visit the university and college websites. You could also look at options in another country, for example the UK or the US.

If you are interested in the UK go to:
www.ucas.com

If you are interested in the US go to:
www.collegeview.com

Work in new groups of three or four, according to the subject that you are interested in. For example, if you are interested in engineering, work with others who are also interested in engineering. Look for the following information based on a subject that you are interested in:

- **Entry requirements – what subjects and grades will you need to do this course?**
- **Type of university – what type of campus is it? Is it in a city?**
- **Fees – how much does it cost?**
- **Scholarship/bursary – are there any scholarships or bursaries? How do you apply?**
- **Housing – what type of accommodation is there?**
- **Extracurricular activities**
- **Study abroad programmes**
- **Any other information of interest**

From the information collected, choose one university or college. **Design** a poster that includes all the information you have found and **present** this to your class.

Vote on the best poster – the one you find most persuasive.

> **Hint**
> Use Glogster to combine images, video, music, photos and audio to **create** a multimedia poster. Visit this website: www.glogster.com

Task 2

In pairs or groups, copy and complete the table below. Think about the kinds of jobs you would like to have in the future, the skills you will need and what you need to do to get there.

Now	5 years	10 years	15 years
School:	School/ College/ University:	Career:	Career:
Skills:	Skills:	Skills:	Skills:
Goals:	Goals:	Goals:	Goals:

◆ Assessment opportunities

◆ This activity can be assessed using Criterion C: Communicating in response to spoken and/ or written and/or visual text and Criterion D: Using language in spoken and/or written form.

▼ Links to: Individuals and societies

'Work around the world' project

In pairs, **discuss** common practices, routines, expectations and values in the workplace for your region or country.

Then research work environments in another culture.

Using a table, **compare and contrast** your country's practices with those of other cultures. You could use the following headings:

• Government benefits including insurance and holiday/leave time

• Workday hours

• The working week

• Opportunities for both men and women

• Childcare options for working parents

• Taxes

• Salary range versus cost of living

Discuss your findings and vote on the best country to live in.

EXTENSION

Using an internet search engine, research the skills that will help to make you future-ready and how they are linked to the changing nature of the world of work. **Identify** the skills that you are confident in and those you would like to develop.

Think about your school subjects and **select** which ones can provide opportunities for you to develop your chosen skills.

In pairs, **discuss** how prepared you feel for the future.

■ Companies use a variety of methods to recruit new graduates, and those in their final year at university

❗ Take action

❗ Did you know that universities, colleges and future employers will do their research on candidates and this means they will look at your profile on social media? How does your social media profile look?

❗ Check your profile using a table like the one below. Start by completing the middle column.

Answer the questions below based on your profile	Examples from your social media profile	Action to take
What are you doing in your profile photo? In other photos?		
Read your last ten posts/comments. **Describe** them.		
Read your 'about' or 'open' section. **Summarize** this.		

❗ What kind of image are you portraying? What kind do you want to portray? Now complete the right-hand column of your table.

❗ Use the information in your table to edit your social media profile to make it more attractive to universities, colleges and future employers.

❗ Delete any parts that are not appropriate.

A SUMMATIVE TASK TO TRY

Use this task to apply and extend your learning in this chapter. This task is designed so that you can evaluate your learning in the Language acquisition criteria.

THIS TASK CAN BE USED TO EVALUATE YOUR LEARNING IN CRITERION A AND CRITERION D TO PHASES 1–2

- Vist this website and watch the video: **www.bbc.co.uk/education/clips/z8bfb9q**
- Then answer the following questions, using your own words as much as possible.
- Do not use translating devices or dictionaries for this task.
- You will have 60 minutes to complete this task.

1 What does Maggie Aderin-Pocock do?　　(strand i)
2 What does Maggie say about school?　　(strand i)
3 **Identify** the difficulty Maggie had as a learner.　　(strand i)
4 Who is the target audience for this programme? **Justify** your answer by stating which features/aspects of the programme are particularly suited to this audience.　　(strand ii)
5 According to Maggie, what is the most important skill to have to do this job?　　(strand iii)

6 What did Maggie study at university?　　(strand i)
7 **Analyse** why Maggie says she is not what 'people expect her to be'.　　(strand ii)
8 Maggie mentions two different routes, or pathways, into science. **Identify** what they are and how they are different.　　(strand ii)
9 Basing your answer on the final part of the video (1.58 onwards), how successful do you think Maggie is? **Explain** your answer by referring to information in the video.　　(strand iii)
10 What does Maggie say she would say to 'little Maggie' if she could travel back in time?　　(strand i)
11 Imagine you are about to finish secondary school: which type of course would you choose and why?　　(strand iii)
12 Which route would suit you: university or a practical course? Why?　　(strand iii)
13 Maggie is very talented and unique. One of the questions she was asked during the interview was, 'What would your superpower be?' Her response was, 'To travel at the speed of light.' Imagine that you wake up one day to discover that your greatest weakness is now a superpower. **Describe** what that superpower would be. (strand iii)
14 Write a 100–150-word paragrpah about what makes you different from other people you know. How do you think this will affect your life? (strand iii)

Reflection

In this chapter we have looked at the **purpose** of the IB learner profile and Approaches to Learning and how they help us to develop the skills that we need to be lifelong learners. We learnt about some careers and how they **connect** to our own talents. Most importantly, we have learnt that, even though we can't predict the future, it's never too early to start thinking about it and how it can shape our **identities and relationships**.

Use this table to reflect on your own learning in this chapter					
Questions we asked	Answers we found	Any further questions now?			
Factual: What is the IB learner profile?					
Conceptual: What kind of learner are you? What careers interest you? How does the Middle Years Programme (MYP) prepare you for university or college?					
Debatable: Which learner profile attributes do you possess? What skills can you develop to help you prepare for the future? How do you know what you want to do with the rest of your life? What would be your dream job?					
Approaches to learning you used in this chapter:	Description – what new skills did you learn?	How well did you master the skills?			
		Novice	Learner	Practitioner	Expert
Communication skills					
Collaboration skills					
Organization skills					
Reflection skills					
Information literacy skills					
Critical-thinking skills					
Creative-thinking skills					
Transfer skills					
Learner profile attribute(s)	Reflect on the importance of being a good inquirier for your learning in this chapter.				
Inquirers					

② What's that you said?

The language we use is a means of **personal and cultural expression**, but for effective **communication** we need to adapt our use of words and phrases to suit different **contexts** and **purposes**.

CONSIDER THESE QUESTIONS:

Factual: What is slang? What is register?

Conceptual: How does street language evolve? How do we change the way we speak in different contexts? How does slang both shape and reflect culture?

Debatable: How much slang is there in my language and how acceptable is its usage? What place does street language have in society?

Now **share and compare** your thoughts and ideas with your partner, or with the whole class.

■ Language can be used differently in different contexts

IN THIS CHAPTER, WE WILL …

■ **Find out** what slang is and how language changes.
■ **Explore** how slang is used in everyday life and in literature.
■ **Take action** to celebrate the way in which we can use slang but also ensure that we can adapt our language for different context and purposes.

'All slang is metaphor, and all metaphor is poetry.' – Gilbert K. Chesterton

'My mother wouldn't allow me to speak slang when I was growing up. But when I got outside, around my friends, it was "Yo" and "That's the joint" and "Yo, what's up?" So I had my game for my friends and my game for my mom.' – Queen Latifah

'I think the problem with people, as they start to mature, they say, "Rap is a young man's game," and they keep trying to make young songs. But you don't know the slang – it changes every day, and you're just visiting. So you're trying to be something you're not, and the audience doesn't buy into that.' – Jay-Z

■ These Approaches to Learning (ATL) skills will be useful …

- ■ Communication skills
- ■ Information literacy skills
- ■ Creative-thinking skills

● We will reflect on this learner profile attribute …

- ● Communicators – we share and receive ideas and information in more than one language.

◆ Assessment opportunities in this chapter:

- ◆ **Criterion A:** Comprehending spoken and visual text
- ◆ **Criterion B:** Comprehending written and visual text
- ◆ **Criterion C:** Communicating in response to spoken and/or written and/or visual text
- ◆ **Criterion D:** Using language in spoken and/or written form

KEY WORDS

audience	neutral	street language
colloquial	register	teen speak
formal	slang	
informal	Standard English	

Have you ever listened to a song or watched a film and felt confused because you didn't understand what they were saying? Well, it might be because they were using **slang**, that is, **informal** or **colloquial** language.

ACTIVITY: Slang dictionary

■ ATL

- ■ Creative-thinking skills: Create original works and ideas

It's amazing to see how internet words are having such a tremendous impact on the English language.

In pairs, look at the acronyms, that is, words that have been abbreviated, in the image and see how many you know. Carry out a search to find the meaning of the ones that are unfamiliar to you. How many did you guess?

Make a list of any English **colloquial** or slang phrases that you know. Visit this website for a slang dictionary to check your examples: http://onlineslangdictionary.com
Add new ones to your list.

Why not **create** your very own class slang dictionary? Try adding words of your own.

In pairs, **discuss**:
- ● **Why is slang such a controversial topic?**
- ● **How much slang is there in your language and how acceptable is its usage?**
- ● **When do you use slang?**

'Colloquial language' is just another way of saying 'everyday speech'.

Learning slang words can be exciting and fun. It helps you communicate and **understand** how people naturally use words and expressions in everyday conversations. It's great when you learn a new word or phrase and find just the right moment to use it. Watching films in English is a good way of learning colloquial and slang expressions. Magazines are also an excellent resource as they're usually written in an informal, chatty style – perfect for improving your conversational English.

What is slang?

HOW DO WE CHANGE THE WAY WE SPEAK IN DIFFERENT CONTEXTS?

Do we always speak in the same way? The answer to this question is simply no, we do not speak to our friends, family or indeed teachers in the same way. As language users, we constantly interact with different people and adjust (change) our language accordingly. In addition, when we start to learn a new language, everyone seems to speak so fast! It is difficult to keep up with all the new words and phrases that we are hearing.

The **register** is the style of language used in different situations. Deciding which register is appropriate to use depends on several things. The relationship between the speaker or writer and their audience will influence the register that is used. If the speaker or writer knows the audience well, then informal, colloquial or slang is appropriate. If we do not know the audience, then we usually use a formal register.

The register that we use also depends on the **context** and **purpose** of what we are saying or writing. Using an informal register in a formal situation is inappropriate because it could seem disrespectful or rude, but using formal language in an informal situation could sound unfriendly. For example, a conversation with your teacher about something that happened during break time would be very different from a conversation with your friends about the same incident.

Formal **Standard English** is the name given to the kind of English you are taught to write in school. Standard English is the language that newsreaders, textbooks, the TV and the radio use. It makes clear communication possible for people from many different cultures and places.

ACTIVITY: How do young Brits speak today?

■ ATL

- Communication skills: Read critically and for comprehension

Visit the following website and read the article:
http://learnenglishteens.britishcouncil.org/uk-now/read-uk/slang

Now answer the following questions. Where possible, provide examples from the text to support your answers.

- **Do young Brits speak like their parents?**
- **Identify the factors that influence how young people speak. Do you agree that these factors are influential? Why? Why not?**
- **What do some UK singers do when they are singing?**
- **Why is it not possible to make a complete list of modern slang?**
- **Interpret the head teacher's decision to ban slang at a school in Sheffield. Do you agree or disagree with the ban?**
- **How does your school feel about students using colloquial language or slang?**
- **Identify the largest group of people speaking English in the world.**
- **According to the text, is it important to learn slang? Why? Why not?**

◆ Assessment opportunities

- ◆ This activity can be assessed using Criterion C: Communicating in response to spoken and/or written and/or visual text and Criterion D: Using language in spoken and/or written form.

Slang, or **street language** as it is sometimes called, is changing all the time and that is why it can be difficult to keep up with all the new words. We are so good at speaking and listening that we do lots of interesting things without really being aware that we are doing them. Let's explore some of these things.

Did you know that most people think that
Dr Johnson invented the dictionary, but Robert
Cawdrey was the first to publish what is called the
Table Alphabeticall in 1604. It was the first single-
language English dictionary ever published. Visit the
British Library website to see what it looked like:
www.bl.uk/learning/timeline/item102970.html

ACTIVITY: UK expressions and slang

■ ATL

■ Communication skills: Write for different purposes

Task 1

In pairs, match the expression or slang word with the Standard
English definition.

Slang	Standard English
ace	call me
cheeky	run
cheerio	brilliant
chivvy along	amazed
do	cool
doddle	not to be trusted
dodgy	hello (to someone you haven't seen in some time)
give us a bell	terrific
gobsmacked	a party
grub	high class
hiya	uncool
hunky-dory	food
leg it	friend
long time no see	rude
mate	cheap
naff	bonkers, crazy, mad
not my cup of tea	goodbye (in a friendly way)
off your trolley	talking about
on about	well-dressed
peanuts	thanks
posh	hurry up
smart	easy
smashing	hello
ta	to talk on and on about nothing
waffle	not to my liking

Visit these websites to check
your answers:

**www.thesaurus.com/browse/
ace?s=t**

http://onlineslangdictionary.com/

Task 2

In pairs, **create** dialogues using
phrases and slang from the list.
Add your own expressions too
and take turns to role play your
dialogue to your classmates. Give
each other feedback and decide
which dialogue is the best.

Here is an example:

A: Hiya, mate!

B: Long time no see.

A: What've you been up to?

B: Not much.

◆ Assessment opportunities

◆ This activity can be assessed
using Criterion D: Using
language in spoken and/or
written form.

ACTIVITY: Everyday English phrases

When we learn new words with no context it is difficult to keep them in our long-term memory, and we sometimes do not understand how to use the word.

To start, in pairs, **discuss**:
- **How do you feel about learning new words?**
- **What strategies do you use to help you learn new words?**
- **If you want to find the meaning of a new word, what do you do?**

Task 1

The best way to learn new words is by using them. So, let's practise some everyday English phrases.

Vist this website, 'The English We Speak', and listen to the short clips for the phrases listed in the box below: **www.bbc.co.uk/worldservice/learningenglish/language/theenglishwespeak/**

butter up	use your loaf
cheesed off	full of beans
pie in the sky	take with a pinch of salt

In groups of three, copy out the following sentences, filling in the gaps with the expressions you have learnt:
- **He can't be trusted and you have to _____ what he says _____.**
- **My little brother is so _____; he loves the seaside!**
- **The service at the restaurant was not good, and my father was really _____ with the waiter.**
- **Latoya tried to _____ the Science teacher to get a higher grade.**
- **Giuseppe has had another accident on his bike. His father told him to start to _____ his _____.**
- **The president of the football team has to offer more than _____ to motivate his players.**

What do all these expressions have in common?

Task 2

You will have guessed that the phrases in the previous task all include a 'food' word.

In groups of three, revisit the website 'The English We Speak' and **select** six new phrases. Listen to the clips and then **create** your own tasks to practise and learn the phrases. Swap tasks with other groups in your class and see how many you get right.

◆ Assessment opportunities

◆ This activity can be assessed using Criterion D: Using language in spoken and/or written form.

Appropriate register

We now know that the register we use is influenced by the purpose of the writing or speech and the audience that it is aimed at. An informal register will use colloquial language and a formal register will use Standard English. But what other things can we look for in an informal register?

When we use an informal register we can use **contractions**, that is, two words that are made shorter to become one. For example, *do not* becomes *don't*. It is important to remember to use an apostrophe to show where there are letters missing.

Another feature of informal writing is to express **how we feel** and our **opinions**. This can be achieved by using a **chatty and friendly tone**. **Humour** is another feature of informal language.

Also, we will use the **first person**, that is: *I, me, my, we* and *our*. Finally, the sentences will be **simple and short**.

Look at this example of informal language:

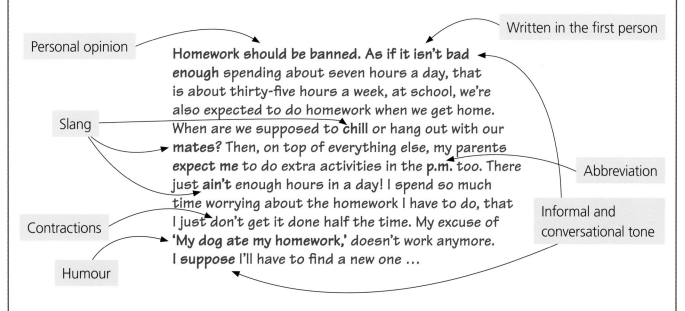

In pairs, rewrite the paragraph using a formal register. Remember that formal writing uses an impersonal tone and does not use a conversational style.

Still confused? Visit this website and go over the differences between informal and formal language: **www.youtube.com/watch?v=sdDBY2-Wmis**

■ All cultures have different concepts of formailty which can be confusing when you start to learn a new language

■ Some contexts require more formal language than others

English for the IB MYP 3: *by Concept*

ACTIVITY: Recognizing formal and informal language features

In pairs, read the following sentences, and decide if each one is informal or formal:

1 Guys, do you wanna come over to my house and play video games later?
2 Would you be interested in watching a film later?
3 Do you wanna a guarantee for your new phone?
4 Would you be interested in purchasing a guarantee with your new phone?
5 Can I get a burger and fries?
6 I'd like a hamburger and fries, please.
7 She was unable to complete her homework on time.
8 She couldn't do the work.
9 Well, we could go tomorrow.
10 It's possible that the weather will allow us to travel tomorrow.
11 You know, the homework is a lot harder than it looks.
12 According to many students, the homework was much more difficult than it first appeared.
13 You could call your doctor if you feel sick.
14 The doctor should be notified if the patient's health deteriorates.
15 I think that was a silly excuse.
16 The reasons provided were unsatisfactory.
17 Boy, I'm starving!
18 I am very hungry.

EXTENSION: EXPLORE FURTHER

In pairs, **explore** further and carry out some research to discover when slang was first used in your country. Give a 2–3-minute presentation to your classmates and answer any questions they may have.

So far in this chapter we have learnt about informal and formal registers and the role they play in helping us to communicate effectively in different contexts. We have tried to develop an understanding of some of the ways our language changes and how consistent we are in the way we use language.

DISCUSS

In pairs, **discuss** the following:
● Do you have similar slang words and expressions in your language?
● How is your language influenced by other languages?
● Some people say that people who use slang are not educated. Do you agree?
● How difficult is it to use slang in a foreign language?
● Do you need to use slang to communicate with non-native speakers?

How does slang both shape and reflect culture?

■ Does slang prevent young people from being able to communicate properly?

HOW MUCH SLANG IS THERE IN MY LANGUAGE AND HOW ACCEPTABLE IS ITS USAGE?

Shakespeare invented more words than most people realize. It is estimated that he introduced more than 1500 different words and phrases into the English language. When he couldn't find the word he needed, he simply created his own. The words Shakespeare invented have become part of our culture and many believe they form the foundation of modern English language. Many of his words are so common that you've probably already quoted Shakespeare today without even realizing.

In many ways, this is similar to what rappers do today and how street language evolves. Shakespeare used the language that was popular with the people at the time, and singers, rappers, poets and young people do the same thing. Language is the result of the society we live in. As a society changes, so does its language. People often make assumptions and judgements based on how people speak. They may assume that the way we speak indicates our position in society.

Teen speak is nothing new. Every generation has had its own language and young people use it to express their independence. It is an expression of their cultural identity and a way to show that they are different from their parents.

Let's **explore** what some of these attitudes are.

ACTIVITY: Horrible Histories William Shakespeare Song

■ ATL

■ Information literacy skills: Access information to be informed and inform others
■ Communication skills: Take effective notes in class

POLONIUS: What do you read, my lord?

HAMLET: Words, Words, Words.

WILLIAM SHAKESPEARE

■ William Shakespeare wrote in what is known as Early Modern English – you might be surprised to find out that it is similar to the English of today

Did you know that about 1000 new words are added to the dictionary every year? And that more than 4000 words are created every year?

Visit this website and read the article 'How new words are born' by Andy Bodle to find out more: www.theguardian.com/media/mind-your-language/2016/feb/04/english-neologisms-new-words

Task 1

Visit this website and see how many of the Shakespearean phrases you can write down: www.youtube.com/watch?v=65Cy4-rfd24

Task 2

In pairs, think of a colloquial word. Use the internet to trace the meaning of your word to its origin. Make notes on the relationship between the word and culture. You can make notes in your own language.

Use a mind map tool like MindMup to **present** your word: www.mindmup.com

Task 3

In groups of three, have a go at making your own Shakespearean insults. Visit this website and choose a word from each column: www.pangloss.com/seidel/shake_rule.html

Decide who has created the best insults.

◆ Assessment opportunities

♦ This activity can be assessed using Criterion C: Communicating in response to spoken and/or written and/or visual text and Criterion D: Using language in spoken and/or written form.

ACTIVITY: From the mouths of teens

■ ATL

■ Communication skills: Paraphrase accurately and concisely; Read critically and for comprehension

1 **Use an online dictionary to find definitions of the following words:**

dialect	teen speak
accent	**Cockney**
multicultural English	

2 **Look at the definitions you have found. Identify any similarities or differences between them.**
3 **Read this article entitled 'From the mouths of teens' and interpret the title of the article:** www.independent.co.uk/news/uk/this-britain/from-the-mouths-of-teens-422688.html
4 **Find words in the text that mean:**

harming	correct
varied	forbidden
identify	extensive

5 **Read this article entitled 'Mind your slanguage':** http://news.bbc.co.uk/1/hi/magazine/8388545.stm
6 **Interpret how the principal at Manchester Academy feels about slang. Make reference to the text in your answer.**
7 **What do you think 'innit' means?**
8 **What does 'in your face' mean?**
9 **Synthesize what you have learnt in the two articles and use it to create a poster about teen speak.**

◆ Assessment opportunities

♦ This activity can be assessed using Criterion C: Communicating in response to spoken and/or written and/or visual text and Criterion D: Using language in spoken and/or written form.

■ Pearly Kings and Queens first appeared in 1875 and still exist today – they wear mother of pearl buttons on their suits and dresses, and have a language of their own, called Cockney

▼ Links to: Individuals and societies – History

A Cockney is a person from a traditional working class area of east London. People who live in this part of London speak in a certain way.

In groups, find out more about the Cockney accent and what it means to be a Cockney:

• When and how did it start?

• What is the connection between this way of speaking and society?

• What is the social attitude to the Cockney accent?

• Is there something similar in your language? Do you have a regional or social accent?

Make a short (2–3-minute) documentary film about Cockney.

Use the links below to help you carry out your research.

www.ukstudentlife.com/Ideas/Fun/Wordplay. htm#Cockney

www.youtube.com/watch?v=XBjp1oEZcwU

www.youtube.com/watch?v=XRVVCbXmYJo

http://thepearlies.co.uk/home/the-history-of- the-pearlies/

COLOUR–SYMBOL–IMAGE

■ ATL

■ Creative-thinking skills: Practise visible thinking strategies and techniques

Lemon Andersen is an American poet, spoken word artist and actor. He uses slang and colloquial language to bring his poems to life.

Task 1

Listen to the TEDYouth 2011 Talk 'Please don't take my Air Jordans' by Lemon Andersen: **www.ted.com/talks/lemon_andersen_performs_ please_don_t_take_my_air_jordans**

As you listen, make notes of things that you find interesting, important or insightful. You can make notes in your mother tongue. You can also click on the subtitles to help you follow the talk. When you finish, choose three of these items that most stand out for you.

• **For one of these, choose a *colour* that you feel best represents or captures the essence of that idea.**

• **For another one, choose a *symbol* that you feel best represents or captures the essence of that idea.**

• **For the other one, choose an *image* that you feel best represents or captures the essence of that idea.**

In pairs, share your colour, symbol and image, and give reasons for your choice.

Task 2

Listen to the poem again and make a note of any new slang words you hear.

◆ Assessment opportunities

◆ This activity can be assessed using Criterion A: Comprehending spoken and visual text.

Let's look at phrasal verbs

Phrasal verbs are very common in informal English. Examples include: *turn off*, *pick up* and *run out of*. These verbs consist of a **basic verb + another word or words**. The two or three words that make up a phrasal verb form a short 'phrase', so they are sometimes called 'multi-phrase verbs'. Phrasal verbs are challenging, because the same phrasal verb can mean different things.

Put is a verb. *Put up* is also a verb – a different verb. The two verbs do not have the same meaning, and they behave differently grammatically. You should treat each phrasal verb as a separate verb, and learn it like any other verb. Look at these examples. You can see that there are three types of phrasal verb formed from a single-word verb:

		Verb	Definition	Example
single-word verb		put	to move to or place in a particular position	Put your books on the shelf.
phrasal verb	verb + adverb	put away	It has multiple meanings: to put in the designated place for storage	Put away your mobile phone when you are in class.
	verb + preposition	put by	to save money	I put by some money for my holiday.
	verb + adverb + preposition	put up with	to tolerate or accept something	I put up with my annoying little sister.

Learning phrasal verbs will help you to understand films and songs, and to chat to your English-speaking friends.

They are a feature used in speech and informal writing. Phrasal verbs can be quite tricky as there are no rules to explain how phrasal verbs are formed correctly – all you can do is look them up in a good dictionary. Some phrasal verbs have multiple meanings.

Visit this website to watch the Fast Phrasal comic-strip videos and do the exercises to learn and practise how to use phrasal verbs correctly: **http://learnenglishteens.britishcouncil.org/grammar-vocabulary/phrasal-verb-videos**

▼ Links to: Arts – Music

Song lyrics often contain slang words and expressions. By listening to songs from different time periods, we can get an insight into the slang words that were popular at that time. They also provide an insight into culture trends, fashion and society.

Task 1

- Visit this website and listen to the lyrics for the song *Fun, Fun, Fun* by the Beach Boys, which was released in 1964:
  http://teachrock.org/video/the-beach-boys-fun-fun-fun-1964

- In pairs, translate the following phrases from the song into Standard English expressions. Which ones are still in use today?

cruised	an ace
old man	Indy 500
blasting	guys
T-Bird	wild goose chase
can't stand her	gettin' wise to you
'cause	all through now

- In groups, use the internet to **select** a song from a different decade and note down the slang words used at that time, and what was fashionable.

- Use your research to make a PowerPoint and **present** this to your classmates.

Task 2

Match the song slang with the correct meaning.

Song slang	Standard English
'cuz / 'coz / 'cause	have got to
gonna	I'm not
wanna	going to
gotta	yes
yeah	because
I ain't	want to

▼ Links to: Individuals and Societies

Find out about the 1960s through songs. The 1960s was one of the most dramatic and controversial decades in history, especially in America. Popular music was a powerful cultural, social and economic force during this decade. Through film and television, and the singles and albums of our parents and grandparents, who have experienced the decade first-hand, we can get an insight into the era.

In pairs, research what the best-selling albums of the year for the first half of the 1960s were. Take a look at the lyrics of those songs and identify the main interconnected themes from the period, including civil rights and race relations; the counterculture and New Left; consumerism; the Cold War; Vietnam and the peace movement; women's liberation; and ecological and environmental concerns.

Present your selection to your classmates.

■ The Beach Boys were an iconic 1960s rock band

▼ Links to: Arts – Music

Many of you will be familiar with the conventions of pop music. But, how much do you really know about it? In pairs, carry out some research and build a picture of the chronology and evolution of pop styles. Some of the older styles and artists may be unfamiliar to you. After all, the 1950s and 1960s probably seem like ancient history!

Present an overview of the historical and cultural background to the conventions of pop to your classmates.

Select the correct terminology to describe what's happening in the music.

EXTENSION

The surf sound of the early 1960s was built on the result of different musical traditions that came together to form something new, something that at the time took America by storm.

In pairs, research the different elements of the Beach Boys' surf sound and identify some essential elements of their early music.

ACTIVITY: *Translate* by Benjamin Zephaniah

■ ATL

■ Creative-thinking skills: Create original works and ideas; Use existing works and ideas in new ways

Benjamin Zephaniah was born in Birmingham in the UK, and grew up in Jamaica and the UK. He became famous in the 1980s with his powerful political poetry. He was one of the poets that made dub poetry famous. Dub poetry is a form of performance poetry that evolved from reggae music and is sometimes performed over music.

Task 1

In pairs, read the poem opposite and try to translate it into Standard English.

Task 2

In groups of three, write a poem or spoken-word piece inspired by and performed over a piece of music.

To start, find a piece of instrumental music that inspires you. YouTube will have lots of ideas for this. Search for 'instrumental reggae' or 'instrumental jazz', and **select** your piece of music. As you listen to the music, write words or phrases.

- **How does the music make you feel?**
- **Does it make you think of particular memories or people?**
- **What mood does it put you in?**
- **What colours and images does the music make you think of?**

Now, have a go at writing your poem.

When you have finished, perform your poem to the music you chose and share it with your classmates.

◆ Assessment opportunities

◆ This activity can be assessed using Criterion C: Communicating in response to spoken and/or written and/or visual text and Criterion D: Using language in spoken and/or written form.

■ Benjamin Zephaniah has campaigned for students to have a greater awareness of the different cultures and languages within Britain

Translate

Who will translate
Dis stuff.
Who can decipher
De dread chant
Dat cum fram
De body
An soul
Dubwise?

Wot poet in
Resident,
Wot translator
Wid wot
Embassy,
Wot brilliant
Linguistic mind
Can kick dis,
Dig dis
Bad mudder luvin rap?

Sometimes I wanda
Why I and I
A try so hard fe get
Overstood,
Mek we juss get
Afrocentric,
Dark,
Who in space
Who on eart
Who de hell we writing fa?

Sometimes I wanda
Who will translate
Dis
Fe de inglish?

By Benjamin Zephaniah

! Take action

! In 2015, out of the total 195 countries in the world, 67 nations have English as the primary language of 'official status'. There are also 27 countries where English is spoken as a secondary 'official' language.

! In November 2010 the British Library started a project, which lasted six months, called 'Evolving English: One Language, Many Voices'. They asked people from around the world to record their voices, either saying six words or reading a few sentences from a storybook in English.

! Visit this interactive map and listen to the different accents from around the world: www.bl.uk/evolvingenglish/mapabout.html

! Start a school 'English Language Voices Blog' to publish creative texts written and or recorded by students. The project should aim to present a snapshot of the many ways you speak across your school community. How does speaking a second language change the way we see the world?

■ What motivates us to learn a new language? It is said that English teenagers are the worst in Europe at leaning a second language.

SOME SUMMATIVE TASKS TO TRY

Use these tasks to apply and extend your learning in this chapter. These tasks are designed so that you can evaluate your learning at different levels of achievement in the Language acquisition criteria.

THIS TASK CAN BE USED TO EVALUATE YOUR LEARNING IN CRITERION A TO PHASE 2

Task 1: The World's English mania

- Visit this website and watch the video 'The world's English mania' by Jay Walker. Jay explains why two billion people around the world are trying to learn English. He shares photos and spine-tingling audio of Chinese students rehearsing English – 'the world's second language': **http://ed.ted.com/lessons/the-world-s-english-mania-jay-walker#watch**
- Then answer the following questions, using your own words as much as possible.
- Refer as closely as possible to the video, **justifying** your answers and giving examples when asked.
- Do not use translating devices or dictionaries for this task.
- Answer the questions in English.
- You will have 60 minutes to complete this task.

1 **Identify** what Jay Walker says is the world's newest mania. (strand i)
2 **Explain** in your own words the meaning of the word 'mania'. (strand ii)
3 **Evaluate** what manias can be.
4 **Identify** how many people are trying to learn English around the world. (strand i)
5 When do Chinese students start to learn English? (strand i)
6 Why does Jay say that people want to learn English? Do you agree or disagree? **Justify** your response with information from the text. (strand iii)
7 In two sentences, **identify** the type of audio-visual text that is used and its basic purpose. (strand ii)
8 After viewing the video, **analyse** the way students learn English in China. In your opinion, is this a good way to learn a language? Why? Why not? (strand iii)
9 What is your experience of learning English? (strand iii)
10 What other universal languages are there? (strand i)
11 **Synthesize** the video using your own words. (strand i)

Task 2: Text speak

■ Read the text on page 38 and then answer the following questions, using your own words as much as possible.

■ Refer as closely as possible to the pictures and text, **justifying** your answers and giving examples when asked.

■ Do not use translating devices or dictionaries for this task.

■ Answer the questions in English.

■ You will have 60 minutes to complete this task.

1 In two sentences, **summarize** what this text is about. (strand i)
2 **Describe** the pictures in your own words. (strand i)
3 **Evaluate** why this text has been created. What are some of the features that make you think this (layout, structure, punctuation, choice of words, **repetition**, diagrams and pictures, graphs, choice of **verbs** or adjectives)? (strand ii)
4 'This article is targeting adults.' Do you agree or disagree with this statement? (strand iii)
5 The text tries to give information about the English language. True or false? **Justify** your response with information from the text. (strand i)
6 According to Professor Sutherland, why did people start using acronyms and abbreviations? (strand ii)
7 Look at the picture of the teenagers. What is the meaning behind this picture? (strand iii)
8 What does 'locked-out class' mean? (strand i)
9 **Interpret** what 'antique speak' means. (strand i)
10 What is the message of this text? Do you think it is an important one? Why? (strand iii)
11 **Identify** how young people communicate nowadays. What does the article compare it to? (strand iii)
12 Taylor Mali is the author of a funny poem called 'Totally like whatever, you know?'. The poem is about language and slang. Follow this link to read the poem: **https://taylormali.com/poems/totally-like-whatever-you-know/**

   Choose a slang word or phrase and use it as a prompt to write a 200-word poem. The poem could be about the slang itself or about how we use language. (strand iii)

Text speak designed to keep parents in the dark: English language is changing so fast there are words majority do not understand

- 86 per cent of parents don't understand what their children say via mobile
- For example 'fleek' means good-looking and 'bae' is an affectionate term
- Teenagers also rely on emoticons and smiley faces in messages

You might think you're gr8 with a little txt speak, but the sorry truth is that these abbreviations are already considered 'antique' by today's children.

The English language is transforming faster than at any point in history thanks to mobile phones and social media, according to a leading academic, and teenagers have constructed an entirely new vocabulary that their parents have no chance of understanding.

As soon as older people learn the linguistic rules, the language transforms again, leaving them behind.

'Text language acts as barbed wire for an older generation,' said John Sutherland, professor emeritus at University College London. 'Parents are part of the locked-out class – they are not allowed in.'

Surveying 2,000 famiies, he found that 86 per cent of parents do not understand the majority of terms their children use in mobile or social media communication.

These include almost unfathomable words such as 'fleek', which means looking good, or 'bae' – a term of affection.

The terms and the meanings	
Fleek	Looking good
FOMO	Fear of missing out
Bae	A term of affection
ICYMI	In case you missed it
Deadout	Rubbish or tired
LMK	Let me know
Thirsty	Looking for attention
NSFW	Not safe for work

Professor Sutherland, who carried out the study with Samsung, said many of the older acronyms and abbreviations used in modern communication – such as gr8 and m8 (great and mate) – developed as a response to the character limits of text messages in early mobile phones.

He added: 'However, technological evolution has meant these words are now effectively extinct from the text speak language and are seen as "antique text speak".'

Today's youth are now said to be moving to a more 'pictographic' form of communication with the increasing popularity of emoticons – pictures such as smiley faces.

Professor Sutherland added: 'This harks back to a caveman-form of communication where a single picture can convey a full range of messages and emoticons.'

The research was carried out to mark the launch of the Samsung Galaxy S6.

By Ben Spencer for the Daily Mail, *May 2015*

Reflection

In this chapter we have learnt about how our day-to-day use of language reveals a great deal about our culture and the communities we are part of. We have also thought about how our language changes depending on **context** and who our audience is. In addition to this, we have seen how we can adapt our register for different **purposes** and how our choice of vocabulary and the way in which we pronounce words can be a means of personal and cultural **expression**.

Use this table to reflect on your own learning in this chapter					
Questions we asked	Answers we found	Any further questions now?			
Factual: What is slang? What is register?					
Conceptual: How does street language evolve? How do we change the way we speak in different contexts? How does slang both shape and reflect culture?					
Debatable: How much slang is there in my language and how acceptable is its usage? What place does street language have in society?					
Approaches to learning you used in this chapter:	Description – what new skills did you learn?	How well did you master the skills?			
		Novice	Learner	Practitioner	Expert
Communication skills					
Information literacy skills					
Creative-thinking skills					
Learner profile attribute(s)	Reflect on the importance of being a good communicator for your learning in this chapter.				
Communicators					

 How can we overcome difficult challenges?

○ Our **identity** is affected by the **relationships** we form; building relationships requires good **communication** and **empathy** for others' **points of view**.

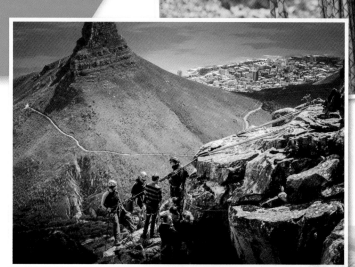

CONSIDER THESE QUESTIONS:

Factual: What is a leader? What is a void?

Conceptual: What is leadership? What does it mean to be a risk-taker? How do you develop leadership skills?

Debatable: When in your life do you feel it is important to take risks? What does it mean to be a leader?

Now **share** and **compare** your thoughts and ideas with your partner, or with the whole class.

■ Sometimes risks can help us develop leadership skills

○ IN THIS CHAPTER, WE WILL ...

■ **Find out** why some people take risks and engage in extreme activities by looking at *Touching the Void* by Joe Simpson.
■ **Explore** different leadership styles.
■ **Take action** by developing our understanding of leadership, learning new skills and growing in confidence as young leaders.

■ **These Approaches to Learning (ATL) skills will be useful ...**

■ Communication skills

■ Collaboration skills

■ Reflection skills

■ Information literacy skills

■ Media literacy skills

■ Critical-thinking skills

■ Creative-thinking skills

■ Transfer skills

● **We will reflect on this learner profile attribute ...**

● Risk-takers – we are not afraid to try new things, even if we're unsure of the outcome.

◆ **Assessment opportunities in this chapter:**

◆ **Criterion A:** Comprehending spoken and visual text

◆ **Criterion B:** Comprehending written and visual text

◆ **Criterion C:** Communicating in response to spoken and/or written and/or visual text

◆ **Criterion D:** Using language in spoken and/or written form

THINK–PAIR–SHARE

Consider these quotes:

'Without risk, we cannot fully appreciate life.' – Anonymous

'A genuine leader is not a searcher for consensus but a molder of consensus.' – Martin Luther King, Jr

'Leadership and learning are indispensable to each other.' – John F. Kennedy

Do you agree or disagree with these statements? Why? Why not? **Discuss** your point of view with a partner.

Consider these questions:

● **Who inspires you?**

● **What is leadership?**

● **What extreme sports or activities do you know of?**

● **What are the most popular extreme sports in your country?**

● **Have you or someone you know tried an extreme sport?**

In pairs, type the word leadership into an internet search engine and see how many results you get. Share what you find with the rest of the class.

Generate a word cloud for 'leadership' using **www.TagCrowd.com** or another tool of your choice.

KEY WORDS

adventure	interview
extreme	leaders
fatal	obstacles
gear	rescue
hazard	risk
injuries	thrill

What is leadership?

HOW DO YOU DEVELOP LEADERSHIP SKILLS?

■ 'Never doubt that a small group of thoughtful, committed people can change the world. Indeed, it is the only thing that ever has.' – Margaret Mead

Have you ever wondered what makes a good leader? What does leadership mean? How does leadership shape our identities and relationships? Well, leadership is all about helping others reach a common goal, how we communicate with others, and our ability to see things from other people's point of view.

ACTIVITY: Word puzzle

■ ATL

■ Creative-thinking skills: Use brainstorming and visual diagrams to generate new ideas and inquiries

LEADERSHIP

Use and rearrange the letters in the word 'leadership' to **create** new words. You can use some or all of the letters in the word to make your new words. How many different words can you come up with?

◆ Assessment opportunities

◆ This activity can be assessed using Criterion D: Using language in spoken and/or written form.

It is not a mysterious attribute that one person has and another does not have. It is learnt behaviour and having the confidence to put these skills into practice. It may surprise you, but leaders are not born; they are developed, almost entirely by their own efforts.

To live happy and fulfilling lives in our society, we need to be able to help ourselves and others to be the best we can be. Learning about the experiences of others teaches us **empathy** and helps us make better-informed choices when we are faced with obstacles. The skills needed to take responsibility for our own actions and to work with other people in achieving goals are part of what we call leadership skills. Leadership is a trait that is unique to the individual. Often, a good leader analyses him or herself to determine in what way he or she can help others.

So, how do you develop leadership skills? They are learnt by observing and listening to others, and through experimentation and practice. Leadership behaviours are the actions used by leaders. Our learning experiences can and do provide us with opportunities to observe and practise leadership skills. At first, we concentrate on performing these actions in specific siuations. Later, as we become comfortable with these behaviours, they become natural to us and part of the leadership skills we use throughout our lives.

ACTIVITY: A lollipop moment

Visit the following website to watch Drew Dudley's talk about 'Everyday Leadership' and then complete the tasks below: www.ted.com/talks/drew_dudley_everyday_leadership

- **Analyse** the title of the TED talk.
- **Evaluate** the speaker's point of view throughout the talk.
- Do you agree or disagree with the speaker? **Justify** your answer.
- In pairs, take turns to **identify** the leadership qualities of one another.
- Have you ever had a 'lollipop moment'? If so, **explain** what it was and how it influenced you.
- Have you ever come across poor leaders in your life? If so, what do you think they could do to improve their leadership qualities?
- **Synthesize** what you have learnt and use it to **create** an advert for 'Inspiring Leaders'.

◆ Assessment opportunities

- ◆ This activity can be assessed using Criterion A: Comprehending spoken and visual text.

ACTIVITY: Write your story, change history

Watch this inspirational TEDYouth 2011 Talk by Brad Meltzer in which he encourages us to dream big, work hard and stay humble, and then complete the tasks below: www.youtube.com/watch?v=9LR7Vb6mqts&t=101s

- What three things does Meltzer tell his children?
- How old was Steve Jobs when he co-founded Apple?
- **Identify** the other famous people mentioned in the talk and write down what they did and how old they were when they did these things.
- How many rejection letters did Meltzer receive when he wrote his first book?
- **Evaluate** Meltzer's description of 'History'. Do you agree with his point of view? Why? Why not?
- Write a 200–240-word essay about a time in your life when you influenced or changed an outcome (how something ended), for example, by starting an environmental squad at school and cutting down on the paper waste.

◆ Assessment opportunities

- ◆ This activity can be assessed using Criterion A: Comprehending spoken and visual text and Criterion D: Using language in spoken and/or written form.

How many results did you find for 'leadership' in the previous task? You probably found about 750 million results on what it means to be a leader, what defines a leader, famous leaders throughout time – in addition to thousands of quotes, tips and comments on leadership skills, and why it's important to possess them! However, what may have surprised you is how little there is to explain leadership to young people and why it's so important for schools and organizations to develop leadership skills in young people. So, the question might be, how do you do it? How do you develop those skills?

A good starting point might be to know yourself – your strengths and weaknesses. Try the mini-questionnaire opposite and see if you can identify with any of the traits.

■ A questionnaire can be described as a 'written interview'

ACTIVITY: Why is it important for us to develop leadership skills?

■ ATL

- Collaboration skills: Give and receive meaningful feedback
- Reflection skills: Consider ATL skills development

In pairs, **discuss**:
- **Do you know what your strengths and weaknesses are?**
- **How good are you at leading?**

A questionnaire is a set of questions on a particular topic that can be completed by an interviewer or by the person who is being asked to answer the questions.

Individually, visit this website and complete the questionnaire, responding to the questions as honestly as you can. The questionnaire encourages you to reflect on how you exercise leadership and take on a variety of roles within groups: **www.mindtools.com/pages/article/newLDR_50.htm**

When you are finished, click on 'Calculate My Total' and share your answers with a partner. How can you use the information from the questionnaire to develop your skills?

Have your answers surprised you? Why? Why not?

◆ Assessment opportunities

- This activity can be assessed using Criterion B: Comprehending written and visual text and Criterion D: Using language in spoken and/or written form.

Interviewing skills

Conducting interviews and asking good questions can be a challenge. Identifying the type of questions to ask can help to develop your interview skills.

Visit this website for interviewing tips and make notes as you watch: **www.youtube.com/ watch?v=SWRYIAfojqk**

Before you interview someone, you need to make a list of all the questions that you would like to ask. Always prepare more questions than you think you will need, just in case – you never know how the interview might go. Remember, open-ended questions are the best type of questions to use.

Open-ended questions are short, simple and have many possible answers. They allow the person being interviewed to provide a detailed answer. These questions begin with a question word: who, what, where, how, why, when or which.

Specific questions enable you to establish factual and historical details. For example, 'How many times did this happen exactly?' and 'When and where were you born?'

Sensory questions bring an interview to life. The idea is to use the senses to add detail. For example, 'What did the battle sound like?' and 'How did the town smell?'

When you have established a connection with the person you are interviewing you are ready to introduce questions that **explore meaning**. These questions reveal feelings, long-term insights and unique personal viewpoints. For example, 'What were your feelings about the election and the results?' and 'What will it mean to you to become the next Prime Minister?'

You should then ask questions for **elaboration and clarification**. For example, 'Can you tell me more about that?' and 'Is there anything else you would like to add?' elicit greater detail and encourage the person you are interviewing to give you more information.

At the conclusion of an interview, encourage a speaker to tell you anything you might have missed in your questions.

Good interviewers are also good listeners and are interested in what the speaker has to say. It's about establishing a connection and remembering that the interview is just a conversation.

Finally, it's a good idea to record your interview – that's what journalists do. It allows you to focus on the give-and-take of the interview, to think on your feet and to be spontaneous in ways that are impossible if you are worried about trying to take detailed notes. But you must ask the person you are interviewing if they are happy for you to record the interview. You can then use your recording to turn your interview into an article.

■ Russian revolutionaries and leaders Joseph Stalin, Vladimir Lenin and Mikhail Ivanovich Kalinin at the Congress of the Russian Communist Party – Stalin (1878–1953) was the Premier of the Soviet Union from 1941 to 1953

For this project you are going to work in pairs and imagine that you have an opportunity to interview famous leaders.

Use a search engine to carry out some research about the **lives and careers of famous world leaders**. **Select** three or four leaders in whom you are interested and be prepared to **explain** why you have selected each of them.

Write a list of questions to ask your leader. You must have a minimum of ten questions.

Consider including at least one question about:

• the leader's background

• how the person became a leader

• what inspired them to become a leader

• a significant contribution for which the leader was responsible

• contributions the leader made

• personal traits and interests.

In your pairs, take turns in the role of interviewer and world leader. Make sure that the questions and answers are historically accurate, and remember that not all leaders have a positive impact. The questions should enable you to share information that you found interesting during the research.

Give each other feedback and say what you found most interesting from the research.

■ Susan B. Anthony and Elizabeth Cady Stanton were the two great leaders of the 19th-century American women's rights movement

■ Swiss humanitarian Henry Dunant (1828–1910) was co-founder of the Red Cross and joint winner of the Nobel Peace Prize in 1901

Visit this website for an example of a useful resource to help you with the task: **www.ducksters.com/biography/**

The ATL skills for research (information literacy skills) require you to:

• Create references and citations, use footnotes/endnotes and construct a bibliography according to recognized conventions

Keep a record of all the sources you have used to support the answers you give during the interview.

ACTIVITY: The IB learner profile and leadership

■ ATL

- Transfer skills: Apply skills and knowledge in unfamiliar situations

Visit this website and review the IB learner profile attributes:
www.youtube.com/watch?v=wqMZ1uXOZ80

Think of some people that you admire; they could be family members, teachers or friends. **Select** one or more people you admire for their leadership skills and write about the IB learner profile attributes that make them unique.

◆ Assessment opportunities

- This activity can be assessed using Criterion C: Communicating in response to spoken and/or written and/or visual text and Criterion D: Using language in spoken and/or written form.

So far in this chapter, we have looked at the qualities that make good leaders and considered the importance of developing leadership skills in preparation for life beyond school. We have also seen that leadership skills can be learnt.

EXTENSION

In pairs, **discuss** the following:
- Does your school have a school council?
- What is the purpose of a school council?
- Is student voice important? Why? Why not?
- **Identify** the skills you can develop through student voice.
- How effective is student voice in your school? Give examples.

Make proposals for students in your school to take a more active role in supporting other's learning and in shaping the student experience both within and outside of your community.

What is a void?

HAVE YOU EVER HAD TO MAKE A REALLY DIFFICULT DECISION?

■ Siula Grande in the Peruvian Andes

In 1985, climbers Joe Simpson and Simon Yates went to the Cordillera Huayhuash in Peru to climb Siula Grande. They succeeded in their attempt to be the first to reach the summit, but their adventure ends in an unexpected way.

So, what does the book *Touching the Void,* by Joe Simpson, which is based on the experiences of the two young mountain climbers, have to do with facing challenges, making difficult decisions and being a resilient leader? To find out, we will analyse extracts from the story and the documentary trailer.

ACTIVITY: Do you judge a book by its cover?

■ ATL

- Communication skills: Interpret and use effectively modes of non-verbal communication

In pairs, search online for the book cover of *Touching the Void* by Joe Simpson. (Hint: Click the images option in your search engine or add images to your search.) Choose your favourite cover. Why did you choose this one? **Discuss** your reasons with your partner.

- What does the cover tell you about the story?
- Does it make you want to read the book? Why? Why not?
- Are you more or less interested in reading books when the story is based on a true event?
- What does 'void' mean? Use an online thesaurus to find synonyms for the word 'void'.

◆ Assessment opportunities

- ◆ This activity can be assessed using Criterion B: Comprehending written and visual text.

Touching the Void was first published in 1988. In 2003 it was turned into an interesting example of a **genre**, called a **docudrama**, directed by Kevin Macdonald. It was awarded the Alexander Korda Award for Best British Film at the 2003 BAFTA Awards.

Filmed in the Peruvian Andes, it includes stunning scenery, a reconstruction of events played by actors and a **narrative** provided by the three men involved: Joe Simpson, Simon Yates and Richard Hawking.

ACTIVITY: Resilience

Read the definition of **RESILIENCE**:

> Having confidence in who you are and what you do, so that you create, build and take opportunities; 'bouncing back', knowing you will find a way through uncertainty, change and even failure.

In pairs, write an **acrostic** about 'resilience', using your own words and including examples to support the ideas in the definition. One line has been done below as an example.

R

E

S

I

Listen to feedback from your teachers to improve your levels of achievement.

I

E

N

C

E

ℹ An acrostic is a poem or a word puzzle in which certain letters in each line form a word or phrase.

◆ Assessment opportunities

◆ This activity can be assessed using Criterion D: Using language in spoken and/or written form.

WATCH–PAIR–SHARE

Think about the purpose of a movie trailer.

Read through the questions below. Then visit this website and watch the trailer for *Touching the Void*. As you watch, make notes to help you answer the questions: **www.youtube.com/watch?v=7Mcdw79l5fQ**

- **When do you find out the title of the film? Why do you think this is?**
- **When do you find out who stars in the film?**
- **Is the music important? Why? Why not?**
- **What type of action from the film do you see?**
- **How does the trailer end?**
- **What clues can you see that help you to identify the genre of the film?**
- **What sport did Joe Simpson and Simon Yates practise?**
- **Write down the words that appear in the trailer. What clues do these words give you about the story?**

In pairs, **discuss** your answers and share your ideas with the rest of the class.

◆ Assessment opportunities

◆ This activity can be assessed using Criterion A: Comprehending spoken and visual text.

ACTIVITY: A question of survival?

Visit the following website to watch a short video showing mountaineers Joe and Simon facing the most difficult challenge of their adventure, and then complete the tasks below: **www.youtube. com/watch?v=pqmYP0OmHcw**

- **Describe** the weather conditions the climbers face in the video.
- What words or phrases in Joe's account bring out most vividly his thoughts and feelings?
- Why did Simon decide to use his penknife to cut the rope?
- **Evaluate** if he made the right decision. Would you have done the same?
- What words or phrases in Simon's account show most clearly the difficult decision he faces? **Explain** carefully the reasons for your choices.
- **Interpret** how Simon felt after he decided to cut the rope.
- How did you feel when you saw the rope had been cut?
- Have you ever had an experience that really frightened you?
- Can you remember a time when you had to make a really difficult decision?
- Write about an adventure in your life that went wrong. What challenges did you face? If something went wrong again, would you do things differently?

◆ Assessment opportunities

◆ This activity can be assessed using Criterion A: Comprehending spoken and visual text and Criterion D: Using language in spoken and/or written form.

ACTIVITY: Touching the Void

Task 1

In pairs, carefully read the two extracts from *Touching the Void* on pages 52–53.

Select one of the accounts and practise writing annotations. Look at the examples on pages 52–53 to help you get started. Use Post-it notes to write down your annotations.

When you have finished, find a pair of students who have focused on the same extract and **discuss** your annotations.

Task 2

In pairs:
- **Interpret** Simon's decision after Joe broke his leg.
- **Analyse** which of the main characters faced the biggest challenges, and what you learnt from the way they respond to what happened.
- **Evaluate** how the language in the texts influences the reader's point of view of how the dangerous situation affected Joe and Simon.

◆ Assessment opportunities

◆ This activity can be assessed using Criterion C: Communicating in response to spoken and/or written and/or visual text and Criterion D: Using language in spoken and/or written form.

Annotating

Annotating means making notes on a text. This will help you to **construct meaning** and remember important things about the text, which you can review and use to complete tasks.

Creating annotations can change a reader's point of view through personal connection with the text.

Remember that you must only use key words as you do not have very much space to write in.

ⓘ Did you know that high winds, snow and dangerous cliffs make Mount Everest one of the most difficult mountains to climb? The current world record holder for the fastest climb is Pemba Dorje Sherpa, with a time of 8 hours and 10 minutes!

ACTIVITY: Discussing themes

■ ATL

- Information literacy skills: Access information to be informed and inform others

You will have realized by now that *Touching the Void* is an intense and powerful story about an adventure.

To help you understand the context and **setting** of the story, carry out some research about Joe Simpson and Siula Grande. Make notes and keep a record of the sources you have used.

Now, find out what happens in the rest of the story. Visit this website to watch the full-length docudrama, *Touching the Void*. Don't forget that you can watch it with subtitles: www.youtube. com/watch?v=QNvBbtUcRkM

In pairs, **discuss** the questions below about the themes that come up in the story. Then prepare a short presentation for your class on the questions that you find most interesting. You can **present** this in the form of a poster or by creating a slideshow on your computer.

- **What makes people take risks and participate in activities like this?**
- **Is survival more important than friendship?**
- **How do you think Joe and Simon's lives changed after their experiences?**
- **What did you learn about mountain climbing from the film?**
- **Do you think Joe and Simon were right to make the climb by themselves? Why? Why not?**
- **Identify the main themes in the story.**
- **Could the accident and the events on the mountain have been avoided?**
- **Analyse any differences in character between Joe and Simon.**

◆ Assessment opportunities

- ◆ This activity can be assessed using Criterion A: Comprehending spoken and visual text, Criterion C: Communicating in response to spoken and/or written and/or visual text and Criterion D: Using language in spoken and/or written form.

Joe's account

I **hit the slope** at the base of the cliff before I **saw it coming**. I was facing into the slope and both knees locked as I struck it. I felt a shattering blow in my knee, felt bones splitting, and screamed. The impact catapulted me over backwards and down the slope of the East Face. I slid, head-first, on my back. The rushing speed of it confused me. I thought of the drop below but felt nothing. Simon would be ripped off the mountain. He couldn't hold this. I screamed again as I jerked to a sudden violent stop.

Everything was still, silent. My thoughts raced madly. Then pain flooded down my thigh – a fierce burning fire coming down the inside of my thigh, seeming to ball in my groin, building and building until I cried out at it, and my breathing came in ragged gasps. My leg! […] My leg!

I hung, head down, on my back, left leg tangled in the rope above me and my right leg hanging slackly to one side. I lifted my head from the snow and stared, up across my chest, at a grotesque distortion in the right knee, twisting the leg into a strange zigzag. I didn't connect it with the pain which burnt my groin. That had nothing to do with my knee. I kicked my left leg free of the rope and swung round until I was hanging against the snow on my chest, feet down. The pain eased. I kicked my left foot into the slope and stood up.

A wave of nausea surged over me. I pressed my face into the snow, and the sharp cold seemed to calm me. Something terrible, something dark with dread occurred to me, and as I thought about it I felt the dark thought break into panic: 'I've broken my leg, that's it. I'm dead. Everyone said it … if there's just two of you a broken ankle could turn into a death sentence … if it's broken … if … It doesn't hurt so much, maybe I've just ripped something.'

I kicked my right leg against the slope, feeling sure it wasn't broken. My knee exploded. Bone grated, and the fireball rushed from groin to knee. I screamed. I looked down at the knee and could see it was broken, yet I tried not to believe what I was seeing. It wasn't just broken, it was ruptured, twisted, crushed, and I could see the kink in the joint and knew what had happened. The impact had driven my lower leg up through the knee joint. […]

I dug my axes into the snow, and pounded my good leg deeply into the soft slope until I felt sure it wouldn't slip. The effort brought back the nausea and I felt my head spin giddily to the point of fainting. I moved and a searing spasm of pain cleared away the faintness. I could see the summit of Seria Norte away to the west. I was not far below it. The sight drove home how desperately things had changed. We were above 19,000 feet, still on the ridge, and very much alone. I looked south at the small rise I had hoped to scale quickly and it seemed to grow with every second that I stared. I would never get over it. Simon would not be able to get me up it. He would leave me. He had no choice. I held my breath, thinking about it. Left here? Alone? […] For an age I felt overwhelmed at the notion of being left; I felt like screaming, and I felt like swearing, but stayed silent. If I said a word, I would panic. I could feel myself teetering* on the edge of it.

Extract from Touching the Void

Simon's account

teetering: to move/balance unsteadily

breaking trail: being in front

trudged: walked or moved slowly and/or with difficulty

crested the rise: reached the top

Joe had disappeared behind a rise in the ridge and began moving faster than I could go. I was glad we had put the steep section behind us at last. […] I felt tired and was grateful to be able to follow Joe's tracks instead of breaking trail*.

I rested a while when I saw that Joe had stopped moving. Obviously he had found an obstacle and I thought I would wait until he started moving again. When the rope moved again I trudged* forward after it, slowly.

Suddenly there was a sharp tug as the rope lashed out taut across the slope. I was pulled forward several feet as I pushed my axes into the snow and braced myself for another jerk. Nothing happened. I knew that Joe had fallen, but I couldn't see him, so I stayed put. I waited for about ten minutes until the tautened rope went slack on the snow and I felt sure that Joe had got his weight off me. I began to move along his footsteps cautiously, half expecting something else to happen. I kept tensed up and ready to dig my axes in at the first sign of trouble.

As I crested the rise*, I could see down a slope to where the rope disappeared over the edge of a drop. I approached slowly, wondering what had happened. When I reached the top of the drop I saw Joe below me. He had one foot dug in and was leaning against the slope with his face buried in the snow. I asked him what had happened and he looked at me in surprise. I knew he was injured, but the significance didn't hit me at first.

No empathy

Cold response

He told me very calmly that he had broken his leg. He looked **pathetic**, and my immediate thought came **without any emotion**. […] You're dead … no two ways about it! I think he knew it too. I could see it in his face. It was all totally rational. I knew where we were, I took in everything around me instantly, and knew he was dead. It never occurred to me that I might also die. I accepted without question that I could get off the mountain alone. I had no doubt about that.

[…] Below him I could see thousands of feet of open face falling into the eastern glacier bay. I watched him quite dispassionately. I couldn't help him, and it occurred to me that in all likelihood he would fall to his death. I wasn't disturbed by the thought. In a way I hoped he would fall. I knew I couldn't leave him while he was still fighting for it, but I had no idea how I might help him. I could get down. If I tried to get him down I might die with him. It didn't frighten me. It just seemed a waste. It would be pointless. I kept staring at him, expecting him to fall …

Extract from Touching the Void

When in your life do you feel it is important to take risks?

WHAT DOES IT MEAN TO BE A RISK-TAKER?

What does risk-taking mean to you? The IB learner profile may aim to develop students who are risk-takers, but risk-taking isn't easy. It encourages us to explore new ideas and innovative strategies, challenge our ways of thinking and be confident in those decisions. This lifelong skill requires us to step out of our comfort zone and become courageous in our choices and actions. This can make us feel anxious at times and afraid to fail. However, facing challenges is a way to become a risk-taker and build our resilience. It pushes us to try things, even hard things, despite the fact that we may not always succeed! Failing becomes an active tool and as the saying goes, 'If at first, you don't succeed, try, try again.' If we can learn to take risks without fear of consequence we also develop our leadership skills and are more open to taking risks in the future, which undoubtedly exposes us to more of the world around us.

ACTIVITY: Unfulfilled dreams

■ ATL

- Communication skills: Take effective notes in class

Sometimes things do not go to plan and the results are different from what you would have liked them to be.

In pairs, visit the following websites to read articles on BMX champion Shanaze Reade and Olympic diver Tom Daley:

> www.theguardian.com/lifeandstyle/2009/jan/11/shanaze-reade-bmx

> www.theguardian.com/lifeandstyle/2009/jan/10/tom-daley-olympics-diving-training

As you read, make notes on when the sports personality started their sport, how much training they do, why they enjoy it, and what they hope to achieve in the future.

In pairs, **discuss**:
- **What are the added pressures of wanting to be very good at a sport when you are still young?**
- **Are sport personalities good role models for young people? Why? Why not?**
- **What leadership skills do they have?**
- **Which IB learner profile attributes would you attribute to Shanaze Reade and Tom Daley?**
- **What challenges do they face?**
- **How are they risk-takers?**

◆ Assessment opportunities

- ◆ This activity can be assessed using Criterion C: Communicating in response to spoken and/or written and/or visual text and Criterion D: Using language in spoken and/or written form.

■ One of the most powerful Approaches to Learning can be found as part of Affective Skills: Resilience – sports people often practise 'bouncing back' after adversity, mistakes and failures

■ Tom Daley found acquiring the mental toughness to compete at the highest level a challenge at first, and admits it is an ongoing process

! Take action

! In groups, **discuss** what it means to *change* something and what it means to *influence* something. Look up both these words in a dictionary or online. Do the definitions help?

! Think about what you might be able to directly change or influence the outcome of. For example, you might be able to stop a local park closing, but can only influence a decision to end poverty throughout your country.

! Is it hard to accept that some things aren't in your control? Are there things you feel you have to accept and can't really expect to change or influence? Being aware and accepting these things can help us to focus on the things we can do.

! **Identify** a cause you feel passionate about and think of specific actions your school community can take.

! What could you achieve in:

   ◆ 10 minutes

   ◆ half an hour

   ◆ an hour

   ◆ a day

   ◆ a week

   ◆ a month?

SOME SUMMATIVE TASKS TO TRY

Use these tasks to apply and extend your learning in this chapter. These tasks are designed so that you can evaluate your learning at different levels of achievement in the Language acquisition criteria.

THIS TASK CAN BE USED TO EVALUATE YOUR LEARNING IN CRITERION B AND CRITERION D TO PHASE 3

Task 1

- Write a 200–250-word interview with *one* of the people in the picture below. What in particular do you want to know about them?
- Take some time to plan your writing. Remember to **organize** your writing using paragraphs.
- Do not use translating devices or dictionaries for this task.
- You will have 60 minutes to complete this task.
- This task will be completed in class under supervision.

■ Climbers Edmund Hillary and Sherpa Tenzing Norgay of the British Everest Expedition celebrate after being the first people to summit Everest, 1953

Task 2: Extreme!

- Write a 200–250-word account for a newspaper, which is featuring a series of articles called 'Extreme!' Write an account of a time when you, or someone you know, experienced the extreme.
- Take some time to plan your writing. Remember to **organize** your writing using paragraphs.
- Do not use translating devices or dictionaries.
- You will have 60 minutes to complete this task.
- It will be completed in class under supervision.

Task 3: Persuasive oral presentation – a sales pitch

Taking part in an expedition requires intense preparation, equipment and supplies. Often these trips are sponsored by large companies. However, the traveller has to convince the company that the trip is worthwhile in order to receive sponsorship.

Imagine you are an explorer. Research and plan a persuasive oral presentation of 3–4 minutes to your future sponsor detailing why you should be given resources (materials and money) to lead an expedition. In your presentation, be sure to cover these points:
- Introduction of who you are (age, nationality, background)
- Why you are qualified to be an explorer (skills and experience)
- What you hope to find on your travels
- What your route will be
- Why you want to explore
- What possible dangers you may experience
- A list of supplies you will need for your trip

Reflection

In this chapter, we have explored experiences of risk-taking, adventure, adversity and endurance. We have seen that triumph of the human spirit and the natural strength we have to succeed often depends on our **communication** with others, and our ability to be open to different **points of view**. Also, we have looked at how the challenges we face shape our **identities and relationships** and that through learning about the experiences of others we can learn **empathy** and be better prepared to overcome challenges.

Use this table to reflect on your own learning in this chapter						
Questions we asked	Answers we found		Any further questions now?			
Factual: What is a leader? What is a void?						
Conceptual: What is leadership? What does it mean to be a risk-taker? How do you develop leadership skills?						
Debatable: When in your life do you feel it is important to take risks? What does it mean to be a leader?						
Approaches to learning you used in this chapter:	Description – what new skills did you learn?		How well did you master the skills?			
			Novice	Learner	Practitioner	Expert
Communication skills						
Collaboration skills						
Reflection skills						
Information literacy skills						
Media literacy skills						
Critical-thinking skills						
Creative-thinking skills						
Transfer skills						
Learner profile attribute(s)	Reflect on the importance of being a risk-taker for your learning in this chapter.					
Risk-takers						

(4) Can we travel through writing?

Travelling to new places allows us to express our **creativity** and gives us access to other **points of view**; the **conventions** of travel writing serve the **purpose** of allowing us to share our experiences with **audiences** from around the world and develop a sense of our **orientation in space and time**.

CONSIDER THESE QUESTIONS:

Factual: What are the conventions of travel writing? What is a travel journal?

Conceptual: Why does travel writing exist? How has travel writing changed over time? What does travel writing reveal about the past? What do we gain from travel writing?

Debatable: Can travel make us better people? Can travel have a harmful effect on our environment? How can we become more responsible travellers?

Now **share and compare** your thoughts and ideas with your partner, or with the whole class.

IN THIS CHAPTER, WE WILL …

- **Find out** what the conventions of travel writing are.
- **Explore** examples of travel writing from across the ages and develop an understanding of how the genre can enrich our lives.
- **Take action** to become responsible travellers and to continue the legacy of travel writing by producing our own work within the genre.

'One's destination is never a place, but always a new way of seeing things.' – Henry Miller

'To travel is to live.' – Hans Christian Andersen

■ These Approaches to Learning (ATL) skills will be useful …

- Communication skills
- Collaboration skills
- Organization skills
- Information literacy skills
- Creative-thinking skills
- Transfer skills

● We will reflect on this learner profile attribute …

- Open-minded – we appreciate our own culture and that of others and listen to other points of view.

◆ Assessment opportunities in this chapter:

- ◆ **Criterion A:** Comprehending spoken and visual text
- ◆ **Criterion B:** Comprehending written and visual text
- ◆ **Criterion C:** Communicating in response to spoken and/or written and/or visual text
- ◆ **Criterion D:** Using language in spoken and/or written form

THINK–PAIR–SHARE

Think about the places you have always wanted to visit. In pairs, make three lists:

- **Places you have always wanted to visit and why you want to visit these places.**
- **Places you have already visited.**
- **Different types of writing associated with travel, for example, a brochure.**

Discuss your lists with a partner.

As a class, try to come up with a definition of what you think travel writing is, in just one sentence.

◆ Assessment opportunities

- ◆ This activity can be assessed using Criterion D: Using language in spoken and/or written form.

KEY WORDS

adventure	journal
brochure	travelogue

What is travel writing?

WHY DO WE READ TRAVEL WRITING?

Whether they be ancient explorers or modern day sightseers, travellers have never been able to resist writing about their journeys. Books, articles and blogs that are used by travellers to record their experiences fall under the genre of travel writing. But the genre isn't limited to descriptive, story-like accounts of people's travels – in fact, it extends to include texts that serve different purposes, such as travel guides and holiday brochures.

Travel books are incredibly popular, and every year millions of them are sold around the world. The popularity of this kind of literature reflects our hunger for travel and exploration and our curiosity about the wider world. Reading about new places, new people and new cultures is not only exciting, but it can also encourage us to become more open minded.

Travel writing can make the big wide world feel like a smaller place. Through the magic of language, travel writers are able to transport us to destinations, both real and imagined, without the need for us to leave the comfort of our armchairs.

In this chapter we will take a journey of our own and learn about the different types of travel writing that exist in the world today.

What are the conventions of travel writing?

WHAT IS A TRAVEL JOURNAL?

What exactly is it that makes travel writing travel writing? The genre is broad and includes a variety of text types. However, there are some conventions that all of these text types share and that bind them together within the same genre.

A good piece of travel writing should evoke feelings of excitement and wonder; it should conjure images of far flung, exotic places or bring to life those that are more familiar; it should inspire readers to pack their bags and venture forth into the world.

So, how does a writer achieve all this? Well, in this section we will find out. Through looking at examples we will learn more about the conventions of travel writing and how writers use language and make certain stylistic choices to make readers feel they are in another world.

ACTIVITY: What does it mean to be a travel writer?

Visit the following website and watch the short video of travel writers Steve Vickerstaff and Kate Humble talking about travel writing, and then complete the tasks below: www.bbc.co.uk/programmes/p00w5s06

1 **Identify** the purpose of the video.
2 According to Vickerstaff, location is the most important thing to consider when travel writing. Is this statement true or false? **Justify** your answer with evidence from the visual text.
3 What is Snowdonia famous for?
4 Humble says that travel writing is subjective. What does she mean by this?
5 **Identify** the three things she always carries with her when travelling.
6 Why are these three things important?
7 What kind of words does she recommend jotting down?
8 In the video she narrates her experiences in typical travel writing style. **Evaluate** how effectively her narration captures her journey.
9 Watch the video again and note down any examples of language or stylistic choices she makes to make her 'writing' richer.
10 **Synthesize** what you have learnt and use it to **create** a poster offering advice to aspiring travel writers.

Did you know that Daunt Books, a chain of bookshops based in London, arrange their books by country?

Navigating your way around their shops is an adventure in itself. Choose a continent or a country and begin browsing.

Founded in 1990, the chain traditionally specializes in travel literature but you can find books of all sorts on their shelves.

Go to the following website to see how their books are arranged: **www.dauntbooks.co.uk/reading-lists**

TAP! Text type, audience and purpose

In pairs, **discuss** what we mean when we talk about the:

- audience for a piece of writing
- purpose of a piece of writing.

When we approach a text for the first time, it is important that we have an understanding of the piece as a whole, a sense of its audience and purpose, and the type of text we're looking at.

When looking at a new text, it is worth asking three important questions:

- What *type of text* is this? Is it a newspaper? A leaflet? A letter?
- Who is the *audience*? Who is the text written for? Teenagers? Adults? Where is the audience? Why might they choose to read this text?
- What is the *purpose* of this text? Why has the writer written this text? What do they hope to achieve? Do they just want to describe their experience? Are they trying to persuade you to do something? Perhaps they are trying to inform or advise about a certain matter.

Look at the texts opposite and **identify** the TAP (text type, audience and purpose) for each one.

EXTENSION

Notice how each text type is different from the others. See if you can **identify** the conventions of each text.

Chapter One

Meet the Family

My Family are the most important people in my life. I love them to bits. Through the bad times and the good times they have always been there for me, especially my mum. It is something the press have managed to twist over the years.

Dear Confused,

You made the wrong decision, so what do you do now? First, you should break off the relationship with your current boyfriend, as you obviously don't really love him.

Maybe you made the wrong choice, but you shouldn't have to live by that for the rest of your life.

Agony Aunt

Ingredients

3 tbsp olive oil

2 sprigs of rosemary, crushed

255 g/8 oz passata (sieved tomatoes)

1 vegetable stock cube

85 ml/3fl oz boiling water

1 tbsp tomato puree

3–4 basil leaves, torn

Method

1 Heat the olive oil in a pan and gently fry the rosemary for 1–2 minutes.

2 Pour in the passata, crumble in the stock cube and add the boiling water and tomato puree.

3 Bring to the boil, reduce the heat and simmer gently for 6–8 minutes.

4 Pour the soup into a bowl and serve, garnished with the torn basil leaves.

Once upon a time, in a land far, far away, a beautiful princess stood at the window of a tall and isolated tower, looking out towards the golden sunset …

How to Give

Amnesty International depends on the support of individuals to carry out its lifesaving work around the world. Every day, we receive more urgent cries for help. Please help make sure we never have to ignore one.

Join Amnesty International

Listening to the news can be unsettling. You may feel helpless when you hear about the inhumanity in the world, but you don't have to feel this way. As a member of Amnesty International, you can do something positive.

Join Us Now …

Body found in search for missing woman

Police investigating the disappearance of a young woman more than three weeks ago have found a body.

Jennifer Drew, 26, from Streatham, south London, was last seen in nearby Croydon in the early hours of 23 May. She had been to a local nightclub with a group of friends.

There are pictures of Miss Drew on CCTV in London Road in Croydon, at 0235 BST, but none of her friends or family have heard from her since.

A body was found on wasteland near Croydon, but has not yet been identified.

As we look at texts in this chapter, **identify** the TAP for each one before exploring it in more depth. It will make things much easier for you.

■ Michael Palin managed to visit 14 countries in 79 days and 7 hours

ACTIVITY: Travel writing conventions

The earliest examples of travel writing took the form of travel journals or travelogues. A travel journal is a chronological, day-by-day, or even hour-by-hour, log or record of one's journey.

Many writers still use this format for their travel writing, including the British actor and writer Michael Palin.

Around the World in 80 Days is a record of Michael Palin's attempt to recreate the **fictional** journey undertaken by Phileas Fogg, the **protagonist** of the French novel, *Around the World in Eighty Days* (*Le tour du monde en quatre-vingts jours*) by Jules Verne. Palin's journey was filmed by a television crew, but the book contains more detail, including Palin's personal views about his experiences.

Palin began his journey on 25 September 1988 and returned 79 days and 7 hours later. He managed to visit 14 countries and covered a total of 28,000 miles!

Opposite is an extract from the book.

Read the extract and answer the questions in the blue boxes.

■ Palin's travels were inspired by Jules Verne's classic novel

Palin varies the lengths of his sentences. Look closely at some examples from the text and consider why he does this.

Travel writing is usually a mixture of research and opinion. Find quotes from the text which are examples of research and opinion.

Facts. The piece includes dates and proper **nouns**: the names of places and organizations. List some more examples of **proper nouns** referred to in the text.

Palin uses stylistic choices to enrich his account. What literary device is being used here? Can you find any other examples?

Day 8: 2 October

Sunday morning in **Cairo**.

I wake with a greater than usual feeling of sensory dislocation. Where am I and what is the horrendous noise? Most of it can be attributed to my air-conditioning unit which changed gear during the night with a splintering crack that sounded as if someone were trying to **batter** the door down.

I silence the air conditioner and throw open the windows only to find there's even more noise outside. I now know why they had laughed at me in reception when I'd asked for a quiet room.

'**In Cairo!**'

I suppose it's sheer weight of numbers. There are over 10 million people living in Greater Cairo and a further million or more unrecorded refugees and squatters – many of them living in the eerily beautiful City of the Dead, a huge and ancient cemetery. I passed by it with fascination, but on enquiry found that cameras are not allowed inside, so, with a day to kill before my next boat connection from Suez, **Passepartout and I** take up the invitation of a man I met in the bar last night to visit an Egyptian movie set. Crossing the Nile by the Tahir bridge I have my first sight of the more **prosperous** side of the metropolis. Hilton, Sheraton and Meridien hotels, skyscraper office blocks. From here Cairo could be anywhere in the world and I'm glad to be at the eccentric Windsor, in the as yet unsmoothed heart of the city.

Extract from Around the World in 80 Days *by Michael Palin*

Travel writing is generally very descriptive. Here Palin uses a variety of **verbs** and **adjectives**. How many others can you find?

Travel writing often contains story-like elements, and here Palin includes direct speech to record conversations he has with people on his journey.

The tone of the piece is relatively informal, even conversational at times. What effect might this have on the audience?

Humour is a great way of engaging readers. Here Palin makes a reference to a character from Verne's novel for comic effect.

Travel writing is often, but not always, written in a chronological order. The text begins with Palin waking up and follows his day from then onwards.

ACTIVITY: Picture perfect

■ ATL

- Organization skills: Select and use technology effectively and productively

In the video you watched on page 63, travel writer Kate Humble says that she finds it helpful to think of writing a piece in terms of pictures. For her, a new picture is a new paragraph.

Photographs can be a great source of inspiration for you as a writer, and can help you to set the scene in the opening of your piece of travel writing.

In pairs, look at the images below and oppostite and, for each one, write a list of ten words you could use to describe the settings.

Turn your lists into a word cloud using a word cloud generator such as **www.wordle.net**.

◆ Assessment opportunities

◆ This activity can be assessed using Criterion C: Communicating in response to spoken and/or written and/or visual text and Criterion D: Using language in spoken and/or written form.

EXTENSION

Select one of the images and use some of the words you have generated to write the opening sentences of a piece of travel writing.

■ Tropical beach

■ Doha in Qatar

■ Cinque Terre in Italy

■ Havana in Cuba

■ Oshino in Japan

Dar es Salaam *Is the capital of German East Afric*

■ Roald Dahl travelled to Dar es Salaam in Tanzania in 1938 for work – he recorded his experience in his memoir *Going Solo*

ACTIVITY: Dar es Salaam

■ ATL

- Communication skills: Read critically and for comprehension; Write for different purposes
- Information literacy skills: Access information to be informed and inform others

In pairs, **discuss**:

- **what you know about the children's writer Roald Dahl**
- **which books you've read by him, if any, and what you enjoyed most about them.**

Although remembered for his children's books, Dahl wrote a great many other things in his lifetime. He was well travelled and wrote about some of his life experiences in his memoir *Going Solo*.

Task 1

Read the extract opposite taken from *Going Solo*, and then answer the following questions. Where possible, provide examples from the text to support your answers.

1 **Identify** as many travel writing conventions in the text as you can.
2 The extract is full of references to colour. **List** all the colours (including different shades) that appear in the extract.
3 What does the word *teeming* mean?
   a busy or crowded
   b working together
   c noisy
4 From the following list, **identify** which word is the odd one out:
      vast   miniscule   immensely   tremendous
   Explain your choice. What do the other words have in common?

5 In the text, find a synonym for the odd word out that you identified in Question 4.
6 Look at the examples below and **identify** the stylistic choices the writer has made:
   a 'and breakers were running up on to the sand'
   b 'coconut palms with their little green leafy hats'
   c 'a great tangle of tremendous dark-green trees'
7 The narrator sees a church and a mosque. What does this tell you about Dar es Salaam?
8 Read lines 26 and 27. What stylistic choices can you **identify**? **Analyse** the line and **explain** what the effect of this is.
9 **Interpret** how the narrator feels about his view of Dar es Salaam. Make reference to the text in your answer.
10 How is England presented in contrast? Make reference to the text in your answer.

Task 2

Use an internet search engine to find out more about Dar es Salaam. Look for factual information that travellers might find useful.

Task 3

Use Dahl's account and the information you have gathered to produce a holiday brochure for the city. Use the box on *Brochures and leaflets* on page 71 to help you.

◆ Assessment opportunities

◆ This activity can be assessed using Criterion B: Comprehending written and visual text, Criterion C: Communicating in response to spoken and/or written and/or visual text and Criterion D: Using language in spoken and/or written form.

Dar es Salaam by Roald Dahl

When I woke up the next morning, the ship's engines had stopped. I jumped out of my bunk and peered through the port-hole. This was my first glimpse of Dar es Salaam and I have never forgotten it. We anchored out [5] in the middle of a vast rippling blue-black lagoon and all around the rim of the lagoon there were pale-yellow sandy beaches, almost white and breakers were running up on to the sand, and coconut palms with [10] their little green leafy hats were growing on the beaches, and there were casuarina trees, immensely tall and breathtakingly beautiful with their delicate grey-green foliage. And then behind the casuarinas was [15] what seemed to me like a jungle, a great tangle of tremendous dark-green trees that were full of shadows and almost certainly teeming, so I told myself, with rhinos and lions and all manner of vicious beasts. [20] Over to one side lay the tiny town of Dar es Salaam, the houses white and yellow and pink, and among the houses I could see a narrow church steeple and a domed mosque and along the waterfront there was [25] a line of acacia trees splashed with scarlet flowers. A fleet of canoes was rowing out to take us ashore and the black-skinned rowers were chanting weird songs in time with their rowing. [30]

The whole of that amazing tropical scene through the porthole has been photographed on my mind ever since. To me it was all wonderful, beautiful and exciting. And so it remained for the rest of my time [35] in Tanganyika. I loved it all. There were no furled umbrellas, no bowler hats, no sombre grey suits and I never once had to get on a train or a bus.

Extract from Going Solo *by Roald Dahl*

Brochures and leaflets

Sometimes known as a pamphlet, a brochure is a small booklet containing pictures and information about a product or service. A leaflet, is very similar in terms of content, but is usually presented on a single sheet of paper rather than over a number of pages.

While the primary purpose of a brochure or leaflet is usually to inform, there is often a secondary purpose to persuade the reader to do something. Follow these tips to write your own:

- Before you start, you need to be clear about who your target audience is so you can tailor your language and tone to suit their needs.
- Think carefully about layout. How are you going to organize the information on your page in an eye-catching and accessible way? Clear, bold headings, subheadings, pictures and captions are all common features of brochures and leaflets.
- Where possible, directly address your readers using personal and inclusive **pronouns** (you, we, us).
- Make sure you include relevant content and factual information – think about what information your readers will need before they can buy into what you are promoting.
- Include direct quotes from people who have used the service or product you are promoting to make it seem more authentic and appealing.
- Include **imperatives** to encourage your readers to take action ('Book your tickets today …')
- Don't forget to include contact details (address, telephone number, website or email address). Invent these details. Never use your own.

Still unsure? Next time you're out and about, see if you can pick up some brochures or leaflets from travel agents, restaurants (or almost anywhere) for more ideas.

So far in this chapter we have looked at what travel writing is and explored the conventions of the genre. We have learnt how writers use language and make certain stylistic choices to bring distant worlds to life for the enjoyment of their audiences. We have also attempted to write our own travel writing texts for different purposes.

How has travel writing changed over time?

WHAT DOES TRAVEL WRITING REVEAL ABOUT THE PAST?

■ One of the earliest examples of travel writing comes from the Greek geographer, Pausanias

Although travel writing as a genre gained popularity in the Victorian era, the earliest examples we have date as far back as the second century. It seems, as humans, we have always had an insatiable thirst for adventure and this is reflected in the vast body of travel writing we have amassed over time.

Even in bygone eras, when transport was nowhere near as efficient as that which we have at our disposal today, people traversed vast distances to seek out new places and new experiences. No ocean was too wide, no mountain too high for the ambitious travellers whose accounts we can still read today.

The Victorian era saw a great many improvements in transport and technology, making it easier for men, and indeed women, to travel than ever before. People were exposed to things they had never encountered before and were eager to record their experiences in writing.

Reading historical travel writing can provide us with an insight into people's attitudes and values in times past, and help us learn about the way in which they saw the wider world. Through looking at examples of travel writing from different periods, we are able to see how much these attitudes have changed over time and begin to develop an understanding of how we became the globalized community we are today.

THE CUNARD LINER "CAMPANIA" AT THE LANDING-STACE, LIVERPOOL.

■ Travel writing as a genre gained popularity in the Victorian era when transport and technology made it easier for people to travel

ACTIVITY: Travelling through time

Look at the extracts taken from different historical periods on pages 74–77.

1 Use the internet to help you fill in the gaps.
2 **Identify** any travel writing conventions in the extracts.
3 **Identify** the main attitudes expressed by the writer in each extract and **interpret** what this reveals about wider social attitudes at the time. How open-minded is each traveller?
4 **Compare** the texts. Can you **recognize** any similarities or differences? What has changed over time? **Discuss** this in pairs or groups.

Some of the original extracts contain **archaic** spellings that make them a little difficult to understand. To make things easier we have adapted the texts so that they are more suited to a modern audience.

● Extract 1: from *The Travels of Sir John Mandeville* by Sir John Mandeville, 1350s
● Extract 2: from *A Brief and True Report of the New Found Land of Virginia* by Thomas Hariot, 1588
● Extract 3: from *A Lady's Visit to the Gold Diggings of Australia* by Mrs Charles Ellen Clacy, 1852–3
● Extract 4: from *Marrakech* by George Orwell, 1939
● Extract 5: from *The Great Railway Bazaar* by Paul Theroux, 1975
● Extract 6: Your turn to choose – using the internet, your school library or even a local bookshop, find an example of travel writing produced in the last five years. Choose a short extract and complete the same tasks as you have done for the previous five extracts.

◆ Assessment opportunities

◆ This activity can be assessed using Criterion B: Comprehending written and visual text and Criterion C: Communicating in response to spoken and/or written and/or visual text.

■ John Mandeville from *The Travels of John Madeville*

■ Native americans in the 1500s

Extract 1

We don't know a great deal about Sir John Mandeville, but in the preface of his book, he calls himself a _____ and claims that he was born and bred in _____. Some people believe that although the travels described in the book are real, John Mandeville might not have been a real person, but rather a **persona** invented by the author of the text.

And then pass men through the isles of Colcos and of Lango, of the which isles Ypocras was lord of. And some men say, that in the isle of Lango is yet the daughter of Ypocras, in form and likeness of a great dragon, that is a hundred fathom of length, as men say, for I have not seen her. And they of the isles call her Lady of the Land. And she lies in an old castle, in a cave, and shows herself twice or three times in the year, and she does no harm to any man, unless men do her harm. And she then changed and transformed, from a fair damsel, into the likeness of a dragon, by a goddess that was clept Diana. And men say, that she shall stay in that form of a dragon, until a knight dares to come to her and kiss her on the mouth; and then shall she turn again to her own kind, and be a woman again, but after that she shall not live long.

Extract from The Travels of Sir John Mandeville *by Sir John Mandeville, 1350s*

What story does Mandeville learn when he is in Lango? He seems to take it very seriously. What does this reveal about people's beliefs at the time?

Extract 2

Thomas Hariot was a cartographer (map maker), mathematician, astronomer and linguist. During the reign of _____, he joined Sir Walter Raleigh to help establish a colony called _____ on Roanoke Island, which is now North Carolina, USA. This piece of travel writing is a report about the native inhabitants and their way of life, particularly their use of a particular plant, called vppówoc.

The vppówoc is of so precious estimation amongst them, that they think their gods are marvelously delighted with it: Because of this sometimes they make hallowed fires & cast some of the powder in for a sacrifice: if there is a storm upon the waters, to pacify their gods, they cast some up into the air and into the water: so a trap for fish being newly set up, they cast some into it and into the air: also after an escape of danger, they cast some into the air: but all done with strange gestures, stamping, sometimes dancing, clapping of hands, holding up of hands, & staring up into the heavens, uttering and chattering strange words & noises.

Extract from A Brief and True Report of the New Found Land of Virginia *by Thomas Hariot, 1588*

What do the verbs and adjectives used by Hariot to describe the native inhabitants of Virginia suggest about what he thinks of them?

Extract 3

In February 1823, gold was discovered in Australia, and sparked a _____, which is a rapid movement of a large number of people to a region where gold has been discovered. People from all over the world travelled to Australia in the hope of making their fortune. Among them was Ellen Clacy, who was born in _____, England. She travelled to Victoria with her _____, and recorded her experiences in writing.

■ People digging for gold in Australia in the 1850s

> What words in the text convey the writer's attitude to the people she encounters on her trip?

I shall not attempt an elaborate description of the town of Melbourne, or its neighbouring villages. A subject so often and well discussed might almost be omitted altogether. The town is very well laid out; the streets (which are all straight, running parallel with and across one another) are very wide, but are incomplete, not lighted, and many are unpaved. Owing to the want of lamps, few, except when full moon, dare stir out after dark.

....

The walking inhabitants are of themselves a study: glance into the streets – all nations, classes, and costumes are represented there. Chinamen, with pigtails and loose trowsers; Aborigines, with a solitary blanket flung over them; Vandemonian pickpockets, with cunning eyes and light fingers – all, in truth, from the successful digger in his blue serge

> Consider the use of listing here. What is the effect?

shirt, and with green veil still hanging round his wide-awake, to the fashionably-attired, newly-arrived 'gent' from London, who stares around him in amazement and disgust. You may see, and hear too, some thoroughly colonial scenes in the streets. Once, in the middle of the day, when passing up Elizabeth Street, I heard the unmistakeable sound of a mob behind, and as it was gaining upon me, I turned into the enclosed ground in front of the Roman Catholic cathedral, to keep out of the way of the crowd. A man had been taken up for horse-stealing and a rare ruffianly set of both sexes were following the prisoner and the two policemen who had him in charge. 'If but six of ye were of my mind,' shouted one, 'it's this moment you'd release him.' The crowd took the hint, and to it they set with right good will, yelling, swearing, and pushing, with awful violence.

Extract from A Lady's Visit to the Gold Diggings of Australia *by Mrs Charles Ellen Clacy, 1852–3*

Extract 4

Born in _____ in 1903, George Orwell is one of the most celebrated writers in the English language. He is known for his essays and novels, the most well known of which include _____, _____ and _____. Throughout his career he travelled extensively and recorded his experiences in vivid detail.

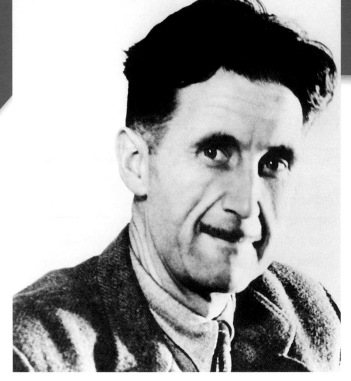

■ George Orwell

Every afternoon a file of very old women passes down the road outside my house, each carrying a load of firewood. All of them are mummified with age and the sun, and all of them are tiny. It seems to be generally the case in primitive communities that the women, when they get beyond a certain age, shrink to the size of children. One day a poor old creature who could not have been more than four feet tall crept past me under a vast load of wood. I stopped her and put a five-sou piece (a little more than a farthing) into her hand. She answered with a shrill wail, almost a scream, which was partly gratitude but mainly surprise. I suppose that from her point of view, by taking any notice of her, I seemed almost to be violating a law of nature. She accepted her status as an old woman, that is to say as a beast of burden.

But what is strange about these people is their invisibility. For several weeks, always at about the same time of day, the file of old women had hobbled past the house with their firewood, and though they had registered themselves on my eyeballs I cannot truly say that I had seen them. Firewood was passing – that was how I saw it. It was only that one day I happened to be walking behind them, and the curious up-and-down motion of a load of wood drew my attention to the human being underneath it. Then for the first time I noticed the poor old earth-coloured bodies, bodies reduced to bones and leathery skin, bent double under the crushing weight.

Extract from Marrakech *by George Orwell, 1939*

How does Orwell bring the people he encounters to life through the use of language? What feelings does he evoke in the reader?

Which learner profile characteristics do you think Orwell possessed, based on your reading of this extract?

Extract 5

The Great Railway Bazaar is the best-known work of American travel writer and novelist Paul Theroux. The travelogue recounts Theroux's _____ month journey across Europe, the Middle East and Asia. When it was first published, the book was a huge success and sold over _____ copies.

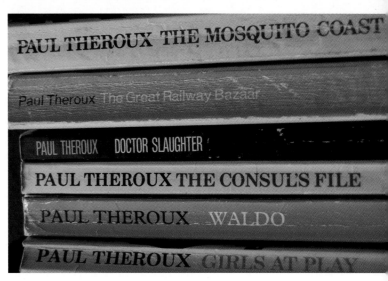

■ Paul Theroux books

My compartment was a cramped two-berth closet with an intruding ladder. I swung my suitcase in and, when I had done this, there was no room for me. The conductor showed me how to kick my suitcase under the lower berth. He hesitated, hoping to be tipped.

'Anybody else in here?' It had not occurred to me that I would have company; the conceit of the long-distance traveller is the belief that he is going so far, he will be alone – inconceivable that another person has the same good idea.

The conductor shrugged, perhaps yes, perhaps no. His vagueness made me withhold my tip. I took a stroll down the car: a Japanese couple in a double couchette – and it was the first and last time I saw them; an elderly American couple next to them; a fat French mother breathing suspicion on her lovely daughter; a Belgian girl of extraordinary size – well over six feet tall,

wearing enormous shoes – travelling with a chic French woman; and (the door was shutting) either a nun or a plump diabolist. At the far end of the car a man wearing a turtleneck, a seaman's cap, and a monocle was setting up bottles on the windowsill; three wine bottles, Perrier water, a broad-shouldered bottle of gin – he was obviously going some distance.

Extract from The Great Railway Bazaar *by Paul Theroux, 1975*

How does Theroux make use of story-like features in the extract to engage his readers?

What do we gain from travel writing?

CAN TRAVEL MAKE US BETTER PEOPLE?

Whether we consume it as readers or produce it as writers, travel literature can enrich our lives in a number of ways. As writers, not only does travel writing allow us to record and share our experiences with others, but it teaches us to reflect on what we perceive; as readers, travel writing gives our minds free rein to wander the earth and learn about new places, people, cultures and much more, without the need to get on a plane.

What it does for both readers and writers alike is to make us all more open-minded. Travel writing breaks down barriers, both geographical and **metaphorical**. Through direct observation and interaction, or indirectly through reading the work of others, we can develop a better understanding of people from across the globe, and celebrate our similarities as well as our differences.

ℹ️ Did you know that the artist Henri Rousseau painted exotic scenes of faraway lands, but never left France? Take a look at some of his work opposite.

While working as a toll collector in Paris, Rousseau taught himself to paint by copying paintings in museums and by sketching plants and animals in the city's botanical gardens and natural history museums.

We could say that Rousseau was an armchair explorer – he used his imagination to travel the world through his paintbrush.

Why not use one of Rousseau's paintings as inspiration for your own travel-writing piece?

ACTIVITY: Travel as therapy

ATL

- Communication skills: Make inferences and draw conclusions
- Creative-thinking skills: Make unexpected or unusual connections between objects and/or ideas

Let us for a moment consider the subject of most travel writing – travel itself. What is the point of travel? What can we gain from it? Let's find out.

Visit the following website and watch the video by The School of Life, and then complete the tasks below: www.youtube.com/watch?v=aaExiKsvt9A

1 **Identify** the purpose of the video.
2 **Who do you think the target audience of the video is?**
3 **Interpret** the message of the video.
4 **What is our 'inner journey'?**
5 **What is the purpose of the 'outer journey'?**
6 **What do you learn about the relationship between religion and travel? What examples does the video use to illustrate this?**

Now, in pairs, **discuss** the following:

- **According to the video, every location in the world contains qualities that can support a beneficial change inside a person. What qualities do you think your country has?**
- **If travel plays such an important role in our personal development, then what does this suggest about the purpose of travel writing?**

◆ Assessment opportunities

- ◆ This activity can be assessed using Criterion A: Comprehending spoken and visual text and Criterion C: Communicating in response to spoken and/or written and/or visual text.

■ Rousseau based his exotic scenes on sketches he made in the botanical gardens in Paris

ACTIVITY: Where shall we go today?

For this activity you'll need a globe. There may be one in your classroom or you may have to borrow one from your Geography teacher.

Task 1: Research

1 Close your eyes and spin the globe.
2 Use your finger to stop the globe from spinning. Don't move your finger when the globe stops moving.
3 Open your eyes, and see where your finger has landed.
4 Using an internet search engine, find out more about the place you have 'selected'. See if you can find some travel guides in your school library that contain the information you are looking for. To make your task easier, you may want to focus on a particular town, city or region. Look for some photographs of the area and learn about the people and the culture.
5 Think about how you can efficiently keep a record of the information you find.

Task 2: Write

It's time to use your imagination.

Once you have gathered enough information about your place, imagine that you have travelled there and write the opening paragraphs of a piece of travel writing.

Think carefully about the tense you use and try to include as many travel-writing conventions as possible.

To help you get started, you can use these questions:

- **How did you get there?**
- **What is likely to be the first thing you see? Describe your surroundings. What do you see? What do you hear? What can you smell?**
- **What are your first impressions of the place? How do you feel?**

Task 3: Evaluate

Share your travel writing with your peers. Swap your piece with a partner and **evaluate** each other's writing.

As you read, check whether or not your partner has used the appropriate conventions. How many features can you **identify**?

◆ Assessment opportunities

♦ This activity can be assessed using Criterion D: Using language in spoken and/or written form.

Can travel have harmful consequences?

HOW CAN WE BECOME MORE RESPONSIBLE TRAVELLERS?

As more and more people pack their bags and set off around the world, we need to reflect on the possible impact this may have on our planet. While most of us strive to be responsible travellers and think carefully about the way in which we behave when we are abroad, tourism nonetheless can have a profound impact on local communities and the environment.

Travel writing inspires us to travel to new places, but it should also teach us the value of our environment and the need to preserve it for future generations. Through reading travel-writing texts we can also gain an understanding of the social norms and etiquette of a place so that we can modify our behaviour (and sometimes our clothing) to respect local customs.

■ The perfect travel companion – a good travel guide can help you get to grips with a new place

ACTIVITY: Travel guides

Unlike much of the descriptive and somewhat narrative travel writing we have explored so far in this chapter, travel guides have an informative purpose. These books contain information about places and offer practical advice on where to stay, what to see, what to eat and how to get around in your chosen destination. The audience for this type of travel writing includes visitors or tourists.

Lonely Planet is the largest travel guide publisher in the world. Since the company was founded over 40 years ago, it has published over 120 million books in 11 different languages. The lively, accessible style of the books has proven popular with travellers worldwide.

Go to a local bookshop or library and find a Lonely Planet guide, or other similar travel guide. Choose an extract from the book (a page or two should be fine) and then complete the following tasks:

1 **Identify** the key similarities and differences between this type of travel-writing text and the others you have explored so far in this chapter.
2 **Infer** what the primary purpose of the text is.
3 **Identify** which features, both visual and textual, the writer has used to achieve this purpose.
4 Who do you think the target audience is?
5 **Identify** examples of typical travel-writing features in the text. For each one, consider why the writer has used them. Not sure what to look for? Use the list below to help you.
   a imperative sentences
   b colloquial language
   c adjectives and verbs
   d proper nouns
   e facts

◆ Assessment opportunities

◆ This activity can be assessed using Criterion B: Comprehending written and visual text.

ACTIVITY: Paradise Lost

Task 1

Read the extract on page 83 from Alex Garland's bestselling novel, *The Beach*, and then **discuss** the following:

1 How is the beach presented in the extract? What kind of place is it? Consider the language used by the writer.
2 This extract is taken from a novel. Does the writer use any travel-writing conventions?
3 What seems to be the beach's most appealing feature?
4 Does the extract make you want to visit such a place? If so, why?

Task 2

The Beach is a story about a young backpacker called Richard who goes travelling in Thailand. When he arrives, he learns of an idyllic beach, untouched by tourism and, with others, sets out to find it.

The novel was hugely successful and became very popular with travellers in particular. It was followed by an equally popular film adaptation, which inspired hoards of travellers to follow in the young protagonist's footsteps for their own taste of paradise.

But what were the consequences of this? Is Garland's idyllic presentation of Thailand still a reality? Read the extract from the article below to find out. As you read, answer the following questions:

1 According to the writer, what does Garland's novel demonstrate?
2 Why was Thailand an ideal location for the story?
3 What were the consequences of the rise in tourism triggered by the film and book?
4 Is it now impossible to find places in the world which have not been destroyed by tourism?
5 According to the writer, why would the novelty of holidaying in an untouched, idyllic destination wear off quite quickly for most travellers?
6 What does the writer suggest has changed about the mindset of travellers in the last decade? Do you think this is true?
7 Why do we need to become more responsible travellers?

Think about a lagoon, hidden from the sea and passing boats by a high, curving wall of rock. Then imagine white sands and coral gardens never damaged by dynamite fishing or trawling nets. Freshwater falls scatter the island, surrounded by jungle – not the forests of inland Thailand, but jungle.

Canopies three levels deep, plants untouched for a thousand years, strangely coloured birds and monkeys in the trees. On the white sands, fishing in the coral garden, a select community of travellers pass the months. They leave if they want to, they return, the beach never changes.

Extract from The Beach *by Alex Garland, 1996*

Thailand: The Beach revisited

Ten years after the release of the film The Beach, *Michelle Jana Chan heads to Thailand to see if paradise can still be found.*

It is one of those rare films that you remember as much for the location as for the star – and that is something given the leading man was Leonardo DiCaprio. Set on the coast of Thailand, the story of The Beach – based on the best-selling book of the same name by Alex Garland – told the tale of travellers' tireless quest for an untouched beach idyll. It also demonstrated how swiftly we can ruin what we find.

Thailand was an ideal location for the story because of its natural beauty but also because the country has a long list of lost paradises. Mass tourism has created hubs of tat and sleaze on once perfect beaches such as Chaweng (an island hop from where Garland set his book) and Koh Phi Phi (where the film was shot). Locals told me they were glad of the income tourism has brought but regretted the arrival of strip joints, drug-fuelled beach parties and cheap sex tourism, which had damaged their conservative, mostly Buddhist culture. The environment has suffered too, evident from murky waters, litter-strewn beaches and the whiff of stagnant drains from side alleys.

Yet in spite of the unrestricted development and crowds, there are seascapes in Thailand forever burnt in my memory for their singular drama: the karstic hills around Krabi, Phuket's sheer cliffs down to sandy coves, the limestone islands rising up from Phang Nga bay. North towards Burma are some of Thailand's finest reefs, offering first-class diving. Remote islands close to Cambodia still retain a traditional rural way of life. And down in the south along the skinny isthmus connecting the country to Malaysia are the whitest of sands – with no hotels in sight.

We might dream of a beach without footprints, but teleport us there and we would drop that idea as quickly as our clothes. The first hour would be bliss, but then we might have a hankering for a long cool drink and the clinking of ice cubes. There would be hunger pangs for a crisp crab salad or grilled squid with lime juice, while we slapped sandflies biting our ankles. After a dip in the sea, it would feel good to rinse under a freshwater shower and dry off with a clean fluffy towel. Then just as we would settle down to watch the sunset (no cocktail in hand), we might be greeted by a cloud of mosquitoes.

Few of us want a truly desert island-style experience. We like our paradises with pest control and pampering. But what has changed in the past decade is that fewer of us want to holiday at the expense of the environment or local culture. In fact, many of us hope our visit and money might support surrounding communities. Cynics will say we are trying to relieve a guilty conscience in a part of the world where the monthly wage is probably less than the price of a massage. Others will add that we are already harming the planet just by flying to our far-flung holiday destination. The latter is certainly true. Nevertheless, holidaymakers have the facts now and are increasingly able to make informed choices – about which kind of hotels we book and about whether to reuse towels and to eat more locally. The environmental and ethical credentials of our holidays increasingly matter. There is no joy in a trip if it ruins paradise in the process. There are too few left.

Extract from The Telegraph, *19 February 2010*

EXTENSION: THE RISE OF THE TRAVEL BLOGGER

Although travel-writing books are still as popular as ever, there is a new breed of travel writer on the scene – the travel blogger.

The internet has made it possible for anyone and everyone to become an author. Being able to post content online gives writers the power and independence to publish their own work and reach a global audience, and as a result, there has been a rise in the number of travel blogs online. Bloggers today have an incredibly wide range of social media platforms from which they can choose to showcase their talent and raise their virtual profile.

But what do you need to do in order to create a successful travel blog? Let's hear from the bloggers themselves …

In pairs, use the internet to find some travel blogs and see what tips their writers have for aspiring travel bloggers. If you get stuck, use the links below:

http://youngadventuress.com/2014/05/make-money-travel-blogging.html

www.worldofwanderlust.com/exactly-how-do-you-become-a-travel-blogger/

www.nomadicmatt.com/travel-blogs/become-successful-travel-blogger/

With your partner, **discuss**:

- As you look through the travel blogs, see if you can **recognize** any patterns. Are there any common or recurring tips?
- Have a look at some travel writing posts. Can you **identify** any travel writing conventions?
- What do you notice about the tone or style of these blogs? What kind of language do the writers use? What effect might this have on readers?

▼ Links to: Individuals and societies – Geography

Tourism can be both a blessing and a curse. Tourism can help boost a country's economy, but also have a devastating effect on the environment.

Visit the following website and **discuss** what you learn about the advantages and disadvantages of tourism: **https://soapboxie.com/economy/Advantages-and-disadvantages-of-tourism**

Is there a lot of tourism in your home country? What tourist attractions are there? What impact does tourism have on:

- the economy
- the environment
- local communities?

If you don't know the answers to these questions, it's time to find out. Use the internet to learn more about tourism in your home country.

! Take action: Opportunity to apply learning through action …

! Become a responsible traveller: Before you set off on your next set of travels, with your family or as part of a school trip, make sure you are well informed about the place. Do your research so you are an open-minded and respectful traveller. While you are abroad, treat the local environment with as much care as you would your own.

! Start your own travel blog: Record your travel experiences online by starting your own blog. You could do this as a class or a year group. Ask a teacher to help you set up the blog and then get writing. Remember, travel is travel – you don't always have to go thousands of miles in order to have a meaningful experience; treat every journey as an adventure worth writing about, even if is just a trip to your nearest seaside.

! Become an armchair explorer: You don't have to leave the comfort of your own home to travel the world. Read, read and read as much travel writing as you can to enhance your understanding of our wonderful and varied world.

SOME SUMMATIVE TASKS TO TRY

Use these tasks to apply and extend your learning in this chapter. These tasks are designed so that you can evaluate your learning at different levels of achievement in the Language acquisition criteria.

THIS TASK CAN BE USED TO EVALUATE YOUR LEARNING IN CRITERION C AND CRITERION D TO PHASE 4

Task 1: Copenhagen

- Read the extract from 'Copenhagen' from *Neither Here Nor There* by Bill Bryson on pages 86–87.
- Then answer the following questions, using your own words as much as possible.
- Refer as closely as possible to the text, **justifying** your answers and giving examples when required.
- Do not use translating devices or dictionaries for this task.
- You will have 60 minutes to complete this task.

1 **Identify** the time of day the narrative is set.   (strand i)
2 What is the weather like? **Identify** examples of language used to demonstrate this.   (strand i)
3 **Identify** an example in the text which suggests that the narrator is being critical.   (strand i)
4 Copenhagen is a beautiful city. Is this statement true or false? Find an example from the text to **justify** your answer.   (strand i)
5 **Analyse** the effect of the narrator's use of adjectives.   (strand ii)
6 **Interpret** how the narrator may have felt at the train station.   (strand ii)
7 Which main tense is used in the text?   (strand ii)
8 What ideas does the narrator express about travelling? Support your answer using evidence from the text.   (strand iii)
9 **Identify** which type of **narrative voice** has been used and **explain** the effect.   (strand i)
10 Bryson is well known for his sense of humour. **Analyse** the use of humour in the text.   (strand iii)
11 What does the **narrator** want us to think about travelling?   (strand ii)
12 **Discuss** how Copenhagen is different from other cities.   (strand i)
13 What does the narrator say you should not do if you travel on a Scandinavian ferry?   (strand i)
14 What effect do you think the narrator was aiming for by using a mix of formal and colloquial language? Support your answer with examples.   (strand ii)
15 How do you like to travel? **Justify** your answer.   (strand iii)

Text adapted: Bill Bryson is travelling through Europe, and has now left Germany for Denmark.

I took a train to Copenhagen. I like travelling by train in Denmark because you are forever getting on and off ferries. It takes longer, but it's more fun. I don't know how anyone could fail to experience that sudden feeling of excitement that comes with pulling up alongside a vast white ship that is about to sail away with you aboard it. I grew up a thousand miles from the nearest ocean, so for me any sea voyage, however brief, remains a novelty. But I noticed that even the Danes and Germans, for whom this must be routine, were looking out of the windows with an air of expectancy as we reached the docks at Puttgarden and our train was moved onto the ferry, the *Karl Carstens*.

Here's a tip for you if you ever travel on a Scandinavian ferry. Don't be the first off the train, because everyone will follow you, trusting you to find the way into the main part of the ship. I was in a group of about 300 people following a confused man in a grey hat who led us on a two-mile hike around the cargo deck, taking us up and down the avenues of railway carriages and huge canvas-sided trucks, casting irritated glances back at us as if he wished we would just go away, but we knew that our only hope was to stick to him like glue and, sure enough, he eventually found a red button on the wall, which when pressed opened a secret hatch to the stairwell.

We reached Copenhagen Central Station at a little after five, but the station tourist office was already closed. Beside it stood a board with the names of thirty or so hotels and alongside each hotel was a small red light to indicate whether it was full or not. About two-thirds of the lights were lit, but there was no map to show where the hotels stood in relation to the station. I considered for a moment jotting down some of the names and addresses, but I didn't altogether trust the board and in any case the addresses were meaningless unless I could find a map of the city.

Perplexed, I turned to find a Danish bag lady clasping my forearm and addressing me in a cheerful babble. These people have an uncanny way of knowing when I hit town. They must have a newsletter or something. We wandered together through the station, I looking distractedly for a map of the city on the wall, she holding onto my arm and sharing crazy confidences with me. I suppose we must have looked an odd sight. A businessman stared at us over the top of a newspaper as we wandered past. 'Blind date,' I explained confidentially, but he just kept staring.

I could find no map of the city, so I allowed the lady to accompany me to the front entrance, where she stopped holding my arm and I gave her some small coins of various nations. She took them and wandered off without a backward glance.

I went to half a dozen hotels in the immediate neighborhood of the station and they were all full. 'Is there some reason for this?' I asked at one. 'Some convention or national holiday or something?'

'No, it's always like this,' I was assured.

Am I wrong to find this exasperating? Surely it shouldn't be too much, on a continent that drives on trade and tourism, to arrange things so that a traveller can arrive in a city in late afternoon and find a room without having to walk around for hours like a boat person. I mean here I was, ready to spend freely in their hotels and restaurants, subsidize their museums and trams, shower them with foreign exchange and pay their extortionate VAT of twenty-two per cent, all without a quibble, and all I asked in return was a place to lay my head.

Like most things when you are looking for them, hotels were suddenly thin on the ground in Copenhagen. I walked the length of the old part of the city without luck and was about to drag myself back to the station to begin again when I came across a hotel by the waterfront called the Sophie Amalienborg. It was large, clean, modern and frightfully expensive, but they could give me a single room for two nights and I took it without hesitation. I had a steamy shower and a change of clothes and hit the streets a new man.

Is there anything, apart from a really good chocolate cream pie and receiving a large, unexpected cheque in the post, to beat finding yourself at large in a foreign city on a fair spring evening, walking slowly along unfamiliar streets in the long shadows of a lazy sunset, pausing to gaze in shop windows or at some church or lovely square or tranquil stretch of quayside, hesitating at street corners to decide whether that cheerful and homy restaurant you will remember fondly for years is likely to be found down this street or that one? I just love it. I could spend my life arriving each evening in a new city.

You could certainly do worse than Copenhagen. It is not an especially beautiful city, but it's an endlessly appealing one. It is home to one and a half million people – a quarter of the Danish population – but it has the pace and ambience of a university town. Unlike most great cities, it is refreshingly free of any ideas of self-importance. It has no monuments to an imperial past and little to suggest that it is the capital of a country that once ruled Scandinavia. Other cities put up statues of generals and potentates*. In Copenhagen they give you a little mermaid. I think that's swell.

Extract from 'Copenhagen,' from Neither Here nor There, *by Bill Bryson*

ⓘ **potentate:** monarchs or rulers

THIS TASK CAN BE USED TO EVALUATE YOUR
LEARNING IN CRITERION C AND CRITERION D TO
PHASE 3

Task 2: Interactive oral

- You will prepare a presentation to **describe** a memorable trip, using the prompts below.
- You will have 10 minutes to prepare for your oral.
- You can make brief notes to help you plan your presentation.
- You are expected to speak for 3–4 minutes.

You should say:

1 where you went
2 how you travelled there
3 who you went with
4 what you did there
5 how long you were there for
6 what made it memorable.

THIS TASK CAN BE USED TO EVALUATE YOUR
LEARNING IN CRITERION C AND CRITERION D TO
PHASE 4

Task 3: Global context – orientation in space and time

Look at the images below and then respond to *one* of the following prompts.

- Imagine you are an individual in one of the images. **Create** a descriptive piece of writing about what is happening, how you feel about it and why.
- **Create** a brochure using one of the images shown. **State** which image you are using.

You will have 45 minutes to complete this task.

Reflection

In this chapter we have learnt about what it takes to be a travel writer and have developed an understanding of the **conventions** of the genre. We have explored the multiple **purposes** travel writing can serve and how writers use language and stylistic choices to transport their **audiences** to faraway lands. In addition, we have seen how, as writers, travel writing can allow us to express our **creativity** through recording our experiences and how, as readers, we can use the genre to access other **points of view**. Through our new-found understanding of travel writing we have developed a sense of our **orientation in space and time** and realized the importance of being responsible and open-minded travellers.

Use this table to reflect on your own learning in this chapter					
Questions we asked	Answers we found	Any further questions now?			
Factual: What are the conventions of travel writing? What is a travel journal?					
Conceptual: Why does travel writing exist? How has travel writing changed over time? What does travel writing reveal about the past? What do we gain from travel writing?					
Debatable: Can travel make us better people? Can travel have a harmful effect on our environment? How can we become more responsible travellers?					
Approaches to learning you used in this chapter:	Description – what new skills did you learn?	How well did you master the skills?			
		Novice	Learner	Practitioner	Expert
Communication skills					
Collaboration skills					
Organization skills					
Information literacy skills					
Creative-thinking skills					
Transfer skills					
Learner profile attribute(s)	Reflect on the importance of being open-minded for your learning in this chapter.				
Open-minded					

5 Is tradition worth preserving?

○ Traditions are an important part of any **culture**, but some can be harmful to certain groups of people. To promote **fairness and development** across the globe, we must allow those without a **voice** to present an **argument** and spread their own **message** about the place of such traditions in the modern world.

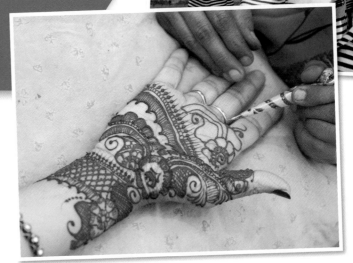

■ 'A people without the knowledge of their past history, origin and culture is like a tree without roots.' – Marcus Garvey

○ IN THIS CHAPTER, WE WILL …

■ **Find out** what traditions are and how they are practised around the world.
■ **Explore** why we hold traditions in such high regard and how they are linked to our cultural identity.
■ **Take action** against harmful traditions and protect those who are vulnerable against dangerous practices.

■ These Approaches to Learning (ATL) skills will be useful …

■ Communication skills
■ Collaboration skills
■ Information literacy skills
■ Media literacy skills
■ Critical-thinking skills
■ Creative-thinking skills

WHAT IS A TRADITION?

Derived from the latin verb *tradere*, which means 'to hand over', the word 'tradition' refers to thoughts, actions or behaviours that are passed down from one generation to the next. Traditions are often tied to religious or cultural beliefs and exist in all cultures.

A tradition can take many forms: it can be as abstract as a thought or attitude or more physical, like a dish or an item of clothing. What all traditions have in common, though, is the fact that they are a reminder of our past and of where we come from. Traditions can allow us to forge a bond with our families, communities and cultures. The traditions we follow can reveal things about our individual identities as well as the issues our ancestors were concerned with; their fears, anxieties and hopes were expressed in traditional practices, established in the past but upheld in the modern world.

Although traditions can make us feel special and safe and give us a sense of belonging, some traditions seem out of place in our modern world, and can even have a

ACTIVITY: What are your traditions?

Use an online dictionary to find the definitions of the following words:

| tradition | ritual | custom | rite | ceremony |

1 Look at the definitions you have found. **Identify** any similarities or differences between them.
2 Use all five definitions to come up with your own definition or explanation of what a tradition is.
3 Write down an example of a:
   a family tradition
   b tradition connected to your faith or another religion
   c tradition from your country or culture
   d tradition that you may have started with your friends.
4 Are there any traditions from your country or culture that are no longer practised? If so, why do you think that is?
5 **Discuss** your answers in pairs and then feed back to the class.

Assessment opportunities

- This activity can be assessed using Criterion C: Communicating in response to spoken and/or written and/or visual text and Criterion D: Using language in spoken and/or written form.

detrimental effect on the physical and emotional well-being of others. Many harmful practices have indeed died out, but some dangerous traditions still exist in our world today.

In this chapter, we will learn more about traditions, their origins and the important purpose they serve but we will also explore whether there is still a place for certain traditions in the modern world.

Why are traditions important?

HOW ARE TRADITIONS CREATED?

Traditions matter to us for many reasons. Whether silly or sacred, traditions are often the source of significant and long-lasting memories for many of us. Traditions not only bring us closer together through celebrating the things that matter most to us, but in a society where we seem to focus more on the future than the past, they provide us with the necessary opportunity to pause and reflect on our histories, both collective and individual.

While many traditions have their roots in religion or culture, some are created in the most unexpected of ways. Anything can become a tradition, as long as there is a commitment made to upholding, following and preserving it. Even going out for pizza with your friends after school once a month can be a tradition.

There are also some traditions we continue to practise without knowing why. The origins of these traditions are not clear to us, yet something keeps us bound to them and they become a part of our lives. Can you think of any traditions you practise without knowing much about their origins?

In this section we will consider why we as humans have such a need for tradition and what it is that makes a tradition a tradition.

■ What traditions matter to you?

ACTIVITY: What makes a tradition a tradition?

 ATL

■ Communication skills: Organize and depict information logically

Read the extracts on pages 93–94 from an article entitled 'Why We Love Traditions, According to Science', and then complete the following tasks:

1 The article is organized using subheadings. In pairs, match the following subheadings to each section of the article:
  a Parents with fun memories of traditions have mentally healthier children
  b We follow traditions because we copy people for safety
  c Powerful traditions have a set of recognized elements

2 **Identify** why traditions 'stick', according to Extract 1. How far do you agree with this idea? **Justify** your opinion.
3 **Identify** the key ingredients of long-lasting traditions according to Extract 2. Can you **apply** these ingredients to a tradition you follow?
4 **Explain** what role sensory information plays in helping to uphold tradition.
5 **Identify** the main idea expressed in Extract 3 on page 94. How far do you agree with this? Make sure you can **justify** your response.

◆ Assessment opportunities

◆ This activity can be assessed using Criterion B: Comprehending written and visual text and Criterion C: Communicating in response to spoken and/or written and/or visual text.

● ● ●

← → C https://www.bustle.com ≡

Why We Love Traditions, According to Science

Extract 1

Human traditions exist, it turns out, largely due to our fear and a determination to do what other people are doing. According to a series of experiments on traditions and imitation conducted in 2015 by the Emotion Lab in Sweden, we're far more likely to obey a tradition (that is, something we observe other people doing) if our choices come with a threat of punishment. We don't follow all traditions just because we enjoy them; subconsciously, we may follow them because we're afraid.

The set of experiments asked participants to choose between two pictures, A and B, on a screen. Participants were then shown a video of someone who picked picture A every time. If participants were told they'd receive an electric shock if they picked the 'wrong' picture, they followed exactly what the person on the video did; but if they were only told they'd be rewarded if they picked the 'right' picture, or that nothing would happen either way, they were a lot less likely to follow the example.

The psychologists behind this experiment think it means that two potent ingredients must combine in order to make a tradition stick: our tendency to copy other people (which is a strong part of human psychology) and our desire to avoid danger. Humans are innate copiers; we even have 'mirror neurons' in our brains to help us ape the movements and speech patterns of those around us. But it seems we're much more likely to stick to copying over generations if we're copying something that is going to keep us out of trouble. So yes, at some point in time, Christmas trees must have protected some of our ancestors from danger.

By J.R. Thorpe

Extract 2

There are, it turns out, four key elements to any tradition or ritual that retains its hold over years – whether it exists just within your family, or is a part of a wider community. These ingredients are: 1. a strictly defined time and place; 2. a set of features that are repeated year after year; 3. another set of features that are different from year to year; and 4. a lot of symbols. Think of Christmas: it's always on December 25, its traditions regarding food and present-giving are pretty set in stone – but every year new elements, like family members or guests, can or be introduced; and it's packed full of symbols, from the tree to the flaming pudding.

It's also psychologically important for the event to contain a lot of sensory information. We tie a huge amount of meaning to memories of sensory information, which is why a whiff of perfume can make you remember a grandmother you barely even met. Traditions that incorporate serious sensory stimulation, from smells to tastes to sounds, are likely to be incredibly powerful psychologically, and to have a lot of significance for us. That roasting-chestnuts smell isn't just for the sake of it.

By J.R. Thorpe

➤

https://www.bustle.com

Extract 3

If your parents absolutely adored the rituals of Christmas, Hanukkah, the winter solstice or whatever they celebrated when they were children, chances are high that you yourself have had more positive interactions with those traditions, and are mentally more stable as a result. According to 2003 research published in Monographs For The Society Of Childhood Development, there's a strong link between parents with positive ideas about traditions and rituals, and how much fun they have with their kids.

It turns out that having enjoyed a happy set of childhood traditions may make your parent more likely to give you support and enact effective rituals for your own time as a kid. That structure and positive reinforcement reduces your risk of developing a mental illness later in life. It's particularly psychologically important to keep up those rituals when children become teens. So if you had a happy childhood, you may be able to credit it in part to your mom's inability to stop dancing to Christmas songs.

By J.R. Thorpe

ACTIVITY: Tradition or superstition?

■ ATL

- Media literacy skills: Demonstrate awareness of media interpretations of events or ideas
- Creative-thinking skills: Make unexpected or unusual connections between objects and/or ideas

It can be difficult to trace the origins of some of the traditions that we still follow today. Superstition, or a belief in the influence of the supernatural, can sometimes give rise to practices which can become traditions.

■ Carved pumpkin lanterns for Halloween

Many people uphold superstitions and related traditional practices without actually understanding why they do so; after all, some of these traditions were established long ago and they may no longer have a place in the modern world where we are able to explain so much through science.

1 In pairs, **discuss** what superstitions have given rise to traditional practices in your culture or country.
2 Listen to the song **Superstition** by **Stevie Wonder** and transcribe the lyrics. (You can pause it in places if you can't keep up.)
3 **Identify** and **list** the superstitions mentioned in the song. Do you know where each of these superstitions came from? Use an internet search engine to find out.
4 **Interpret** the message of the song. **Discuss** this in pairs.

◆ Assessment opportunities

- ◆ This activity can be assessed using Criterion A: Comprehending spoken and visual text and Criterion C: Communicating in response to spoken and/or written and/or visual text.

How can traditions help us develop a sense of personal and cultural identity?

DO TRADITIONS VARY FROM PLACE TO PLACE?

■ Traditions from around the world (from left to right): Japanese tea ceremony; tomato festival in Spain; Indian festival of Raksha Bandhan; rodeo in the USA

Traditions play a key role in helping to shape our identities; they can give us that all-important sense of belonging to a culture or community and give us a means of staying connected to people and places. Being away from home and continuing to practise a tradition can make us feel closer to our loved ones. Which traditions make you feel connected to your country or culture?

Learning about a friend's traditions and even sharing them can be a great way of developing an understanding of their culture and the values which they hold dear. We may practise the same traditions as people from other places but in different ways and this can be a great opportunity to open our minds to new and exciting experiences. Do you share any traditions with your friends? What do you do that is the same – or different? Share and **compare** your experiences.

Traditions that connect us to our cultures can take many forms. We can follow traditions by taking part in festivals, wearing certains types of clothing, eating particular foods or even by interacting with others in a particular way.

In this section we will look at the way we observe traditions around the world and how traditions can make us feel connected (or in some cases disconnected) to our culture.

ACTIVITY: World traditions

ATL

■ Information literacy skills: Access information to be informed and inform others; Present information in a variety of formats and platforms

Which of your culture's traditions do you hold dear? Now's your opportunity to share them with others.

Would you like to learn more about traditions from around the world? Maybe you want to find out about how a common tradition, such as the celebration of a festival, varies from place to place? You may even want to explore traditions from all corners of the Earth and look at traditions that are unique to different regions.

It's up to you how you approach this task as long as by the end of it you produce the following:
- A 3–5-minute presentation. You can choose how you present this (as a poster, PowerPoint presentation, oral presentation, a short film).
- A detailed, narrative description of how one of the traditions you have chosen is carried out.

Remember, your presentation *must* show evidence of extensive research gathered from a variety of different sources.

◆ Assessment opportunities

◆ This activity can be assessed using Criterion D: Using language in spoken and/or written form.

ACTIVITY: Presents from my Aunts in Pakistan

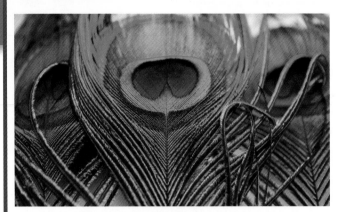

■ 'They sent me a salwar kameez/peacock-blue'

■ 'Candy-striped glass bangles/snapped, drew blood'

Wearing traditional clothing is a simple way of connecting to or celebrating a particular culture. For those of us who find ourselves caught between more than one culture, wearing traditional clothes can sometimes give rise to more complex questions about our identity.

Read the poem on page 97 by Moniza Alvi, a Pakistani-born British writer, and then complete the following tasks:

1 'The speaker feels comfortable in her clothes.' **Evaluate** this statement and **determine** whether it is true or false. **Justify** your answer using two examples from the text.

2 **Interpret** what the poet means by 'a fractured land'.

3 **Infer** what the word 'aflame' in this context means:

   a on fire   c excited

   b embarrassed   d angry.

4 **Analyse** why she feels this way.

5 **Identify** another word in the poem that means bright.

6 Can you **understand** why the poem focuses so much on clothes? **Interpret** what the clothes represent.

7 **Infer** what she is looking for when she looks into the mirrors.

8 How does she perceive the Pakistani culture? Which words in particular convey this?

9 What traditions connect her to Pakistan and how connected or disconnected does she feel to the place and her family there?

10 In pairs, **discuss** whether you can relate to her experience in any way. Are traditional clothes a part of your culture? If so, by wearing them, do you feel more connected to your culture?

! Take action

! Do you ever wear traditional clothes? Why not **organize** a 'Wear traditional clothes day' at your school?

! You could encourage your teachers and peers to wear traditional clothing to school for one day, to fundraise. **Select** a charity of your choice and donate the money you have raised.

! Start by researching the clothing you plan to wear and **explain** to your class the traditions linked to your costume. Either choose clothes from your culture/heritage, or you could research the traditional clothing from another culture: **www.roughguides.com/gallery/traditional-dress/**

Presents from my Aunts in Pakistan

They sent me a salwar kameez
    peacock-blue,
        and another
  glistening like an orange split open,
embossed slippers, gold and black
      points curling.
    Candy-striped glass bangles
      snapped, drew blood.
    Like at school, fashions changed
      in Pakistan –
the salwar bottoms were broad and stiff,
      then narrow.
My aunts chose an apple-green sari,
  silver-bordered
      for my teens.

I tried each satin-silken top –
  was alien in the sitting-room.
I could never be as lovely
    as those clothes –
  I longed
for denim and corduroy.
  My costume clung to me
    and I was aflame,
I couldn't rise up out of its fire,
  half-English,
      unlike Aunt Jamila.

I wanted my parents' camel-skin lamp –
  switching it on in my bedroom,
to consider the cruelty
    and the transformation
from camel to shade,
  marvel at the colours
    like stained glass.
My mother cherished her jewellery –
  Indian gold, dangling, filigree,

But it was stolen from our car.
The presents were radiant in my wardrobe.
  My aunts requested cardigans
    from Marks and Spencers.

My salwar kameez
  didn't impress the schoolfriend
who sat on my bed, asked to see
  my weekend clothes.
But often I admired the mirror-work,
  tried to glimpse myself
    in the miniature
glass circles, recall the story
  how the three of us
    sailed to England.
Prickly heat had me screaming on the way.
  I ended up in a cot
In my English grandmother's dining-room,
  found myself alone,
    playing with a tin-boat.

I pictured my birthplace
  from fifties' photographs.
    When I was older
there was conflict, a fractured land
  throbbing through newsprint.
Sometimes I saw Lahore –
    my aunts in shaded rooms,
screened from male visitors,
  sorting presents,
    wrapping them in tissue.

Or there were beggars, sweeper-girls
  and I was there –
    of no fixed nationality,
staring through fretwork
  at the Shalimar Gardens.

By Moniza Alvi

▼ Links to: Individuals and societies

Did you know that there are a group of women in Namibia who dress as if they were Victorians? What influence does clothing have on society, culture and traditions? Research to find out why some groups wear a certain type of clothing.

Based on your research, write five questions a television reporter might ask if he or she were preparing a feature news story on your subject. In pairs, answer the questions and videotape your interview.

So far we have learnt about traditions and how they help to connect us to our cultures and places of origin. We have tried to develop an understanding of where traditions come from and why we hold on to them long after they have been established.

Can traditions be harmful?

WHY DO WE FOLLOW TRADITION?

Although so far in this chapter we have looked mostly at tradition as a positive, enriching aspect of human life and culture, it is important for us to recognize that some traditions can be harmful, and put the lives of vulnerable people and animals in jeopardy.

The roots of many traditions lie in the past, and while this can connect us to our history and give us an insight into the lives of our ancestors, we must ask whether these customs, established in bygone eras, still have a place in our world today. In the case of many harmful traditions, we have lost the reasoning behind why they came into existence in the first place; or, more significantly, the justifications behind these practices are no longer relevant in the modern age.

In the past, people have been reluctant to take a stand against harmful traditions, or even dare to name them as such. We cannot deny, however, that some traditions are detrimental to the health and emotional well-being of certain groups around the world, and should therefore raise questions about why we continue to carry out these practices.

ACTIVITY: The Lottery

■ ATL

■ Communication skills: Read critically and for comprehension

'The Lottery' is a short story by American writer Shirley Jackson. When it was first published it caused a great deal of controversy.

Task 1

Before you read the story, in pairs, **discuss** the following:
- **What is a lottery?**
- **What do you think the story will be about?**

Task 2

Now read the story on pages 99–105 and then complete the following tasks:

1 **Construct meaning** by making inferences about the following. **Justify** your answers by making reference to the text.
   a When the story was written or set
   b Where the story is set

2 **Identify** and list some of the rules of the lottery which are outlined in the story.
3 **Analyse** the description of the black box in paragraph 5 on page 100. What does it reveal about the tradition of the lottery?
4 **Evaluate** some of the attitudes expressed about the tradition by the characters in the story. How do the old feel about it? Do the young think differently?
5 **Evaluate** why the townspeople did what they did in the story.
6 **Interpret** the message of the story.
7 What do you **understand** about the writer's attitude towards traditional practices?

Task 3

In pairs, take a moment to reflect on the story and **discuss**:
- **your feelings about the message of the story**
- **whether the message applies to any harmful traditions practised in the world today.**

◆ Assessment opportunities

◆ This activity can be assessed using Criterion B: Comprehending written and visual text.

The Lottery

The morning of June 27th was clear and sunny, with the fresh warmth of a full-summer day; the flowers were blossoming profusely and the grass was richly green. The people of the village began to gather in the square, between the post office and the bank, around ten o'clock; in some towns there were so many people that the lottery took two days and had to be started on June 2th, but in this village, where there were only about three hundred people, the whole lottery took less than two hours, so it could begin at ten o'clock in the morning and still be through in time to allow the villagers to get home for noon dinner.

The children assembled first, of course. School was recently over for the summer, and the feeling of liberty sat uneasily on most of them; they tended to gather together quietly for a while before they broke into boisterous play, and their talk was still of the classroom and the teacher, of books and reprimands. Bobby Martin had already stuffed his pockets full of stones, and the other boys soon followed his example, selecting the smoothest and roundest stones; Bobby and Harry Jones and Dickie Delacroix – the villagers pronounced this name 'Dellacroy' – eventually made a great pile of stones in one corner of the square and guarded it against the raids of the other boys. The girls stood aside, talking among themselves, looking over their shoulders at the boys, and the very small children rolled in the dust or clung to the hands of their older brothers or sisters.

Soon the men began to gather, surveying their own children, speaking of planting and rain, tractors and taxes. They stood together, away from the pile of stones in the corner, and their jokes were quiet and they smiled rather than laughed. The women, wearing faded house dresses and sweaters, came shortly after their menfolk. They greeted one another and exchanged bits of gossip as they went to join their husbands. Soon the women, standing by their husbands, began to call to their children, and the children came reluctantly, having to be called four or five times. Bobby Martin ducked under his mother's grasping hand and ran, laughing, back to the pile of stones. His father spoke up sharply, and Bobby came quickly and took his place between his father and his oldest brother.

The lottery was conducted – as were the square dances, the teen club, the Halloween program – by Mr Summers, who had time and energy to devote to civic activities. He was a round-faced, jovial man and he ran the coal business, and people were sorry for him, because he had no children and his wife was a scold. When he arrived in the square, carrying the black wooden box, there was a murmur of conversation among the villagers, and he waved and called, 'Little late today, folks.' The postmaster, Mr Graves, followed him, carrying a three-legged stool, and the stool was put in the center of the square and Mr Summers set the black box down on it. The villagers kept their distance, leaving a space between themselves and the stool, and when Mr Summers said, 'Some of you fellows

➤

want to give me a hand?', there was a hesitation before two men, Mr Martin and his oldest son, Baxter, came forward to hold the box steady on the stool while Mr Summers stirred up the papers inside it.

The original paraphernalia for the lottery had been lost long ago, and the black box now resting on the stool had been put into use even before Old Man Warner, the oldest man in town, was born. Mr Summers spoke frequently to the villagers about making a new box, but no one liked to upset even as much tradition as was represented by the black box. There was a story that the present box had been made with some pieces of the box that had preceded it, the one that had been constructed when the first people settled down to make a village here. Every year, after the lottery, Mr Summers began talking again about a new box, but every year the subject was allowed to fade off without anything's being done. The black box grew shabbier each year; by now it was no longer completely black but splintered badly along one side to show the original wood color, and in some places faded or stained.

Mr Martin and his oldest son, Baxter, held the black box securely on the stool until Mr Summers had stirred the papers thoroughly with his hand. Because so much of the ritual had been forgotten or discarded, Mr Summers had been successful in having slips of paper substituted for the chips of wood that had been used for generations. Chips of wood, Mr Summers had argued, had been all very well when the village was tiny, but now that the population was more than three hundred and likely to keep on growing, it was necessary to use something that would fit more easily into the black box. The night before the lottery, Mr Summers and Mr Graves made up the slips of paper and put them in the box, and it was then taken to the safe of Mr Summers' coal company and locked up until Mr Summers was ready to take it to the square next morning. The rest of the year, the box was put away, sometimes one place, sometimes another; it had spent one year in Mr Graves's barn and another year underfoot in the post office, and sometimes it was set on a shelf in the Martin grocery and left there.

There was a great deal of fussing to be done before Mr Summers declared the lottery open. There were the lists to make up – of heads of families, heads of households in each family, members of each household in each family. There was the proper swearing-in of Mr Summers by the postmaster, as the official of the lottery; at one time, some people remembered, there had been a recital of some sort, performed by the official of the lottery, a perfunctory, tuneless chant that had been rattled off duly each year; some people believed that the official of the lottery used to stand just so when he said or sang it, others believed that he was supposed to walk among the people, but years and years ago this part of the ritual had been allowed to lapse. There had been, also, a ritual salute, which the official of the lottery had had to use in addressing each person who came up to draw from the box, but this also had changed with time, until now it was felt necessary only for the official to speak to each person approaching. Mr Summers was very good at all this; in his clean white shirt and blue jeans, with one hand resting carelessly on the black box, he seemed very proper and important as he talked interminably to Mr Graves and the Martins.

Just as Mr Summers finally left off talking and turned to the assembled villagers, Mrs Hutchinson came hurriedly along the path to the square, her sweater thrown over her shoulders, and slid into place in the back of the crowd. 'Clean forgot what day it was,' she said to Mrs Delacroix, who stood next to her, and they both laughed softly. 'Thought my old man was out back stacking wood,' Mrs Hutchinson went on, 'and then I looked out the window and the kids was gone, and then I remembered it was the twenty-seventh and came a-running.' She dried her hands on her apron, and Mrs Delacroix said, 'You're in time, though. They're still talking away up there.'

Mrs Hutchinson craned her neck to see through the crowd and found her husband and children standing near the front. She tapped Mrs Delacroix on the arm as a farewell and began to make her way through the crowd. The people separated good-humoredly to let her through: two or three people said, in voices just loud enough to be heard across the crowd, 'Here comes your Missus, Hutchinson,' and 'Bill, she made it after all.' Mrs Hutchinson reached her husband, and Mr Summers, who had been waiting, said cheerfully, 'Thought we were going to have to get on without you, Tessie.' Mrs Hutchinson said, grinning, 'Wouldn't have me leave m'dishes in the sink, now, would you, Joe?' and soft laughter ran through the crowd as the people stirred back into position after Mrs Hutchinson's arrival.

'Well, now,' Mr Summers said soberly, 'guess we better get started. Get this over with, so's we can go back to work. Anybody ain't here?'

'Dunbar,' several people said. 'Dunbar. Dunbar.'

Mr Summers consulted his list. 'Clyde Dunbar,' he said. 'That's right. He's broke his leg, hasn't he? Who's drawing for him?'

'Me, I guess,' a woman said, and Mr Summers turned to look at her. 'Wife draws for her husband,' Mr Summers said. 'Don't you have a grown boy to do it for you, Janey?' Although Mr Summers and everyone else in the village knew the answer perfectly well, it was the business of the official of the lottery to ask such questions formally. Mr Summers waited with an expression of polite interest while Mrs Dunbar answered.

'Horace's not but sixteen yet,' Mrs Dunbar said regretfully. 'Guess I gotta fill in for the old man this year.'

'Right,' Mr Summers said. He made a note on the list he was holding. Then he asked, 'Watson boy drawing this year?'

A tall boy in the crowd raised his hand. 'Here,' he said. 'I'm drawing for my mother and me.' He blinked his eyes nervously and ducked his head as several voices in the crowd said things like 'Good fellow, Jack,' and 'Glad to see your mother's got a man to do it.'

'Well,' Mr Summers said, 'guess that's everyone. Old Man Warner make it?'

➤

'Here,' a voice said, and Mr Summers nodded.

A sudden hush fell on the crowd as Mr Summers cleared his throat and looked at the list. 'All ready?' he called. 'Now, I'll read the names – heads of families first – and the men come up and take a paper out of the box. Keep the paper folded in your hand without looking at it until everyone has had a turn. Everything clear?'

The people had done it so many times that they only half listened to the directions: most of them were quiet, wetting their lips, not looking around. Then Mr Summers raised one hand high and said, 'Adams.' A man disengaged himself from the crowd and came forward. 'Hi, Steve,' Mr Summers said, and Mr Adams said, 'Hi, Joe.' They grinned at one another humorlessly and nervously. Then Mr Adams reached into the black box and took out a folded paper. He held it firmly by one corner as he turned and went hastily back to his place in the crowd, where he stood a little apart from his family, not looking down at his hand.

'Allen,' Mr Summers said. 'Anderson … Bentham.'

'Seems like there's no time at all between lotteries any more,' Mrs Delacroix said to Mrs Graves in the back row.

'Seems like we got through with the last one only last week.'

'Time sure goes fast,' Mrs Graves said.

'Clark … Delacroix.'

'There goes my old man,' Mrs Delacroix said. She held her breath while her husband went forward.

'Dunbar,' Mr Summers said, and Mrs Dunbar went steadily to the box while one of the women said, 'Go on, Janey,' and another said, 'There she goes.'

'We're next,' Mrs Graves said. She watched while Mr Graves came around from the side of the box, greeted Mr Summers gravely and selected a slip of paper from the box. By now, all through the crowd there were men holding the small folded papers in their large hand, turning them over and over nervously. Mrs Dunbar and her two sons stood together, Mrs Dunbar holding the slip of paper.

'Harburt … Hutchinson.'

'Get up there, Bill,' Mrs Hutchinson said, and the people near her laughed.

'Jones.'

'They do say,' Mr Adams said to Old Man Warner, who stood next to him, 'that over in the north village they're talking of giving up the lottery.'

Old Man Warner snorted. 'Pack of crazy fools,' he said. 'Listening to the young folks, nothing's good enough for them. Next thing you know, they'll be wanting to go back to living in caves, nobody work any more, live that way for a while.

Used to be a saying about "Lottery in June, corn be heavy soon." First thing you know, we'd all be eating stewed chickweed and acorns. There's always been a lottery,' he added petulantly. 'Bad enough to see young Joe Summers up there joking with everybody.'

'Some places have already quit lotteries,' Mrs Adams said.

'Nothing but trouble in that,' Old Man Warner said stoutly. 'Pack of young fools.'

'Martin.' And Bobby Martin watched his father go forward. 'Overdyke … Percy.'

'I wish they'd hurry,' Mrs Dunbar said to her older son. 'I wish they'd hurry.'

'They're almost through,' her son said.

'You get ready to run tell Dad,' Mrs Dunbar said.

Mr Summers called his own name and then stepped forward precisely and selected a slip from the box. Then he called, 'Warner.'

'Seventy-seventh year I been in the lottery,' Old Man Warner said as he went through the crowd. 'Seventy-seventh time.'

'Watson.' The tall boy came awkwardly through the crowd. Someone said, 'Don't be nervous, Jack,' and Mr Summers said, 'Take your time, son.'

'Zanini.'

After that, there was a long pause, a breathless pause, until Mr Summers, holding his slip of paper in the air, said, 'All right, fellows.' For a minute, no one moved, and then all the slips of paper were opened. Suddenly, all the women began to speak at once, saving, 'Who is it?', 'Who's got it?', 'Is it the Dunbars?', 'Is it the Watsons?' Then the voices began to say, 'It's Hutchinson. It's Bill. Bill Hutchinson's got it.'

'Go tell your father,' Mrs Dunbar said to her older son.

People began to look around to see the Hutchinsons. Bill Hutchinson was standing quiet, staring down at the paper in his hand. Suddenly, Tessie Hutchinson shouted to Mr Summers. 'You didn't give him time enough to take any paper he wanted. I saw you. It wasn't fair!'

'Be a good sport, Tessie,' Mrs Delacroix called, and Mrs Graves said, 'All of us took the same chance.'

'Shut up, Tessie,' Bill Hutchinson said.

'Well, everyone,' Mr Summers said, 'that was done pretty fast, and now we've got to be hurrying a little more to get done in time.' He consulted his next list. 'Bill,' he said, 'you draw for the Hutchinson family. You got any other households in the Hutchinsons?'

➤

'There's Don and Eva,' Mrs Hutchinson yelled. 'Make them take their chance!'

'Daughters draw with their husbands' families, Tessie,' Mr Summers said gently. 'You know that as well as anyone else.'

'It wasn't fair,' Tessie said.

'I guess not, Joe,' Bill Hutchinson said regretfully. 'My daughter draws with her husband's family; that's only fair. And I've got no other family except the kids.'

'Then, as far as drawing for families is concerned, it's you,' Mr Summers said in explanation, 'and as far as drawing for households is concerned, that's you, too. Right?'

'Right,' Bill Hutchinson said.

'How many kids, Bill?' Mr Summers asked formally.

'Three,' Bill Hutchinson said.

'There's Bill Jr, and Nancy, and little Dave. And Tessie and me.'

'All right, then,' Mr Summers said. 'Harry, you got their tickets back?'

Mr Graves nodded and held up the slips of paper. 'Put them in the box, then,' Mr Summers directed. 'Take Bill's and put it in.'

'I think we ought to start over,' Mrs Hutchinson said, as quietly as she could. 'I tell you it wasn't fair. You didn't give him time enough to choose. Everybody saw that.'

Mr Graves had selected the five slips and put them in the box, and he dropped all the papers but those onto the ground, where the breeze caught them and lifted them off.

'Listen, everybody,' Mrs Hutchinson was saying to the people around her.

'Ready, Bill?' Mr Summers asked, and Bill Hutchinson, with one quick glance around at his wife and children, nodded.

'Remember,' Mr Summers said, 'take the slips and keep them folded until each person has taken one. Harry, you help little Dave.' Mr Graves took the hand of the little boy, who came willingly with him up to the box. 'Take a paper out of the box, Davy,' Mr Summers said. Davy put his hand into the box and laughed. 'Take just one paper,' Mr Summers said. 'Harry, you hold it for him.' Mr Graves took the child's hand and removed the folded paper from the tight fist and held it while little Dave stood next to him and looked up at him wonderingly.

'Nancy next,' Mr Summers said. Nancy was twelve, and her school friends breathed heavily as she went forward switching her skirt, and took a slip daintily from the box 'Bill Jr,' Mr Summers said, and Billy, his face red and his feet overlarge, near knocked the box over as he got a paper out. 'Tessie,' Mr Summers said. She hesitated for a minute, looking around defiantly, and then set her lips and went up to the box. She snatched a paper out and held it behind her.

'Bill,' Mr Summers said, and Bill Hutchinson reached into the box and felt around, bringing his hand out at last with the slip of paper in it.

The crowd was quiet. A girl whispered, 'I hope it's not Nancy,' and the sound of the whisper reached the edges of the crowd.

'It's not the way it used to be,' Old Man Warner said clearly. 'People ain't the way they used to be.'

'All right,' Mr Summers said. 'Open the papers. Harry, you open little Dave's.'

Mr Graves opened the slip of paper and there was a general sigh through the crowd as he held it up and everyone could see that it was blank. Nancy and Bill Jr opened theirs at the same time, and both beamed and laughed, turning around to the crowd and holding their slips of paper above their heads.

'Tessie,' Mr Summers said. There was a pause, and then Mr Summers looked at Bill Hutchinson, and Bill unfolded his paper and showed it. It was blank.

'It's Tessie,' Mr Summers said, and his voice was hushed. 'Show us her paper, Bill.'

Bill Hutchinson went over to his wife and forced the slip of paper out of her hand. It had a black spot on it, the black spot Mr Summers had made the night before with the heavy pencil in the coal company office. Bill Hutchinson held it up, and there was a stir in the crowd.

'All right, folks,' Mr Summers said. 'Let's finish quickly.'

Although the villagers had forgotten the ritual and lost the original black box, they still remembered to use stones. The pile of stones the boys had made earlier was ready; there were stones on the ground with the blowing scraps of paper that had come out of the box. Mrs Delacroix selected a stone so large she had to pick it up with both hands and turned to Mrs Dunbar. 'Come on,' she said. 'Hurry up.'

Mr Dunbar had small stones in both hands, and she said, gasping for breath, 'I can't run at all. You'll have to go ahead and I'll catch up with you.'

The children had stones already. And someone gave little Davy Hutchinson a few pebbles.

Tessie Hutchinson was in the center of a cleared space by now, and she held her hands out desperately as the villagers moved in on her. 'It isn't fair,' she said. A stone hit her on the side of the head. Old Man Warner was saying, 'Come on, come on, everyone.' Steve Adams was in the front of the crowd of villagers, with Mrs Graves beside him.

'It isn't fair, it isn't right,' Mrs Hutchinson screamed, and then they were upon her.

By Shirley Jackson

> 'But her greatest assets were her bound feet, called in Chinese "three-inch golden lilies" (san-tsun-gin-lian). This meant she walked "like a tender young willow shoot in a spring breeze," …' from Wild Swans, by Jung Chang

10th century	People in the court of Emperor Li Yiu of the Tang Dynasty are entranced by court dancer Yao Niang's feet, which are bound by white silk to resemble a crescent moon. Many believe that this is where the root of the tradition lies.	900 / 1000
1644	Manchu nobility come into power and try with little success to ban footbinding.	
1874	The first anti-footbinding committee is formed in Shanghai by a British priest.	1600
1912	Footbinding is officially banned by the government of the new Republic of China, which came into being following the Xinhai Revolution of 1911.	1700
1949	Following their rise to power, the Communists issue their own ban on footbinding.	1800
1950	Chairman Mao orders anti-footbinding inspectors to publicly shame any bound women they find.	1900
2009	The last factory producing 'lotus shoes' closes down.	2000

■ Lotus shoes – the last factory producing 'lotus shoes' closed in 2009

■ Lotus feet – a timeline

▼ Links to: Individuals and society – History: Lotus feet

Outlawed in 1911, foot binding was a tradition that was practised by women in China to attain what were known as lotus or lily feet.

Small feet were associated with beauty and refinement – having feet that were considered too large by contemporary beauty standards could have an incredibly damaging effect on a woman's future prospects. Marriage for most women in pre-twentieth century China was their only option and male suitors from wealthy families had a preference for women with lotus feet. To ensure the cultivation of small feet, girls as young as four would have their feet painfully manipulated and bound so that they were ideally no more than four inches long.

Not only were their feet disfigured by the practice, but the women were in constant, agonizing pain throughout their lives as a consequence. Footbinding restricted women's mobility and therefore meant that their participation in society was limited as they found themselves confined to their homes.

You can read more about footbinding and the experiences of women with lotus feet by visiting the following website: **www.theguardian.com/world/2005/mar/21/china.gender**

First, her feet were plunged into hot water and her toenails clipped short. Then the feet were massaged and oiled before all the toes, except the big toes, were broken and bound flat against the sole, making a triangle shape. Next, her arch was strained as the foot was bent double. Finally, the feet were bound in place using a silk strip measuring ten feet long and two inches wide. These wrappings were briefly removed every two days to prevent blood and pus from infecting the foot. Sometimes 'excess' flesh was cut away or encouraged to rot. The girls were forced to walk long distances in order to hasten the breaking of their arches. Over time the wrappings became tighter and the shoes smaller as the heel and sole were crushed together. After two years the process was complete, creating a deep cleft that could hold a coin in place. Once a foot had been crushed and bound, the shape could not be reversed without a woman undergoing the same pain all over again.

Extract from 'Why Footbinding Persisted in China for a Millennium', Smithsonian Magazine

■ Chinese woman with bound feet poses for a photo in the early twentieth century

Task 1

Look at the timeline above and, in pairs, **discuss** the following:

• What can you **infer** from the timeline about the impact this tradition had on the lives of women before and after it was banned? How does it make you feel?

• Although here the origins of the tradition are attributed to Yao Niang's feet, no one really knows where the tradition came from. Use an internet search engine to find out some alternative theories about when or why the tradition began.

• Why then do you think the tradition continued for so long despite there being little certainty about where or why it began? **Evaluate** whether we should continue to follow traditions if their origins are unclear.

Task 2

Read the extract above from a magazine article to learn about the process that was carried out.

Passive voice

Sentences can be in the active or **passive voice**.

Active voice describes a sentence in which the subject performs the action stated by the verb. For example:

- Nicolo ate the cake.

In this case, 'Nicolo', the subject of the sentence, has actively carried out the action stated by the verb 'ate'. It is clear to us as readers that it is Nicolo who has carried out this action, and it is the subject rather than the object (the cake) that is the main focus of the sentence. If you need a reminder about the subject, object and verb of a sentence, go back to Chapter 1 of *English for the IB MYP 1: by Concept*.

Look at the same sentence, this time in the passive voice:

- The cake was eaten by Nicolo.

You will notice that the object is now the subject of the sentence. We don't even have to include 'by Nicolo', even though we know that someone must have had to carry out the action.

When changing the active to the passive voice, we also need to change the tense of the sentence, as shown in the table below.

Tense	Active voice	Passive voice
Present simple	They **sell** sweets here.	Sweets **are sold** here.
Present continuous	They **are serving** lunch.	Lunch **is being served**.
Present perfect simple	He **has delivered** the letters.	The letters **have been delivered**.
Past simple	They **fixed** the car this morning.	The car **was fixed** this morning.
Past continuous	They **were performing** the play at The Globe.	The play **was being performed** at The Globe.
Past perfect simple	She **had left** the note on the table.	The note **had been left** on the table.
Future simple	We **will issue** a fine unless you return the books.	A fine **will be issued** unless you return the books.

We use the passive voice when we want to shift the focus to the 'thing' in the sentence which the action is being done to, or to the action itself.

We also use the passive form if we don't know who is doing the action or if we do not want to mention who is doing the action.

For example, look at the following:

- I haven't done my homework. (active)
- My homework hasn't been done. (passive)

What might be the advantage of using the passive voice to break this news to your teacher?

Newspapers often use the passive voice, especially for headlines. Can you think why?

To find out more or to practise the passive voice, visit the following website: **https://learnenglish. britishcouncil.org/en/english-grammar/verbs/ active-and-passive-voice**

EXTENSION

ATL

- Communication skills: Read critically and for comprehension

Take another look at the extract about foot-binding on page 107.

1 **Explain** why the passive voice has been used in this case.

2 If you were to change the text from the passive to the active voice, who do you think would be the subject of the sentences (that is, who carried out the act of foot binding)? Use an internet search engine to find out.

3 Change the passage from the passive to the active voice. Consider the effect of this.

◆ Assessment opportunities

- ◆ This activity can be assessed using Criterion C: Communicating in response to spoken and/or written and/or visual text and Criterion D: Using language in spoken and/or written form.

ACTIVITY: Talking tradition

ATL

■ Collaboration skills: Listen actively to other perspectives and ideas

Task 1

In pairs, **discuss** the quotes on this page and page 111 about tradition.

- **Interpret** what each quote means.
- **Analyse** the thoughts, feelings, ideas or attitudes about tradition that are being expressed in these quotes.
- Can you **recognize** any patterns? What do they all have in common?

Task 2

Synthesize your ideas and write a paragraph about how people feel about tradition.

◆ Assessment opportunities

◆ This activity can be assessed using Criterion C: Communicating in response to spoken and/or written and/or visual text and Criterion D: Using language in spoken and/or written form.

'Tradition becomes our security, and when the mind is secure it is in decay.' – Jiddu Krishnamurti

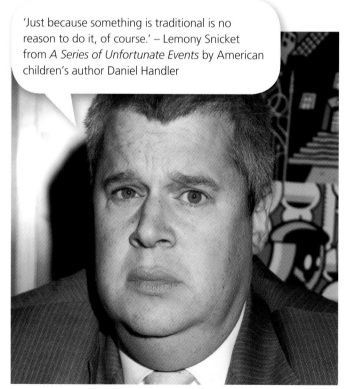

'Just because something is traditional is no reason to do it, of course.' – Lemony Snicket from *A Series of Unfortunate Events* by American children's author Daniel Handler

'The less there is to justify a traditional custom, the harder it is to get rid of it.' – Mark Twain

'Tradition is a fragile thing in a culture built entirely on the memories of the elders.' – Alice Albinia

'Tradition does not mean a dead town; it does not mean that the living are dead but that the dead are alive.' – G.K. Chesterton

'When a tradition gathers enough strength to go on for centuries, you don't just turn it off one day.' – Chinua Achebe

Is it OK to compromise the safety of animals for the sake of tradition?

■ Each year, thousands of animals are subjected to cruelty for the sake of tradition

In some cultures and religions around the world, certain animals are revered and even worshipped in the form of gods or deities. For centuries, animals have taken centre stage in certain traditional practices, yet, tragically, their safety and rights have often been overlooked, and many have suffered as a result.

Today, as a society, we are more sensitive to the needs of animals than people were in the past. We understand that animals are complex creatures and appreciate the important role they fulfil in our world. Over the years, we have developed laws to protect animals from cruelty. Yet, in some parts of the world, hundreds of animals each year are used in festivals where they are subjected to inhumane treatment.

Unlike us, animals do not possess a voice which allows them to express the injustice they suffer for the sake of tradition. How do you feel about this issue? Is tradition a reasonable justification for animal cruelty?

Do you know of any traditional festivals or practices from your country or culture in which animals are used?

ACTIVITY: Don't support bullfighting

■ ATL

- Communication skills: Make inferences and draw conclusions
- Collaboration skills: Listen actively to other perspectives and ideas

Although the origins of bullfighting can be traced back to ancient Mesopotamia (a large area now known to us as Iraq, Syria and part of Turkey) and the Mediterranean, since medieval times the practice has become synonymous with Spain and the Spanish culture.

You can find out more about bullfighting by visiting the following website for the League Against Cruel Sports, a charity dedicated to putting an end to cruel practices often carried out in the name of tradition: www.league.org.uk/bullfighting-and-bull-running

Supporters of bullfighting say it is an integral part of the national culture. But is it right to sacrifice animals for the sake of tradition?

Task 1

Look at the poster on the opposite page and then complete the following tasks:

1 **What is the element that caught your attention first in this poster? Why?**

PATRICIA DE LEÓN
PARA PeTA

LA TRADICIÓN NO ES UNA
EXCUSA PARA LA CRUELDAD

NO APOYE
LAS CORRIDAS
DE TOROS

2 **Identify** the kind of organization that has produced this image and the purpose of the poster.

3 Can you **recognize** any links between the image and the text beneath it?

5 **Interpret** the message the creator is trying to convey.

6 **Identify** the visual and textual clues that illustrate how the creator's message has been presented in this poster. **Evaluate** how effectively this message has been conveyed. You do *not* have to refer to the text in the image in your answer.

7 **Infer** who you think this message is addressed to.

8 **Analyse** the effect of the colour red used in the image. Does it represent anything in particular?

Task 2

Some people say that bullfighting should continue because it is important to preserve traditions. Do you agree or disagree with this statement? **Explain** why.

How could you convince people to stop bullfighting or cruelty to animals in general? In pairs or groups, **create** a mind map of the ways in which you could raise awareness of the cause.

◆ Assessment opportunities

◆ This activity can be assessed using Criterion B: Comprehending written and visual text.

'Celebrating our culture is very important to me. But one thing I cannot support is the senseless killing of animals in bullfights. From the moment the bull enters the ring, he's destined to die. Outnumbered, frightened, even drugged or injured, his death will be slow and painful.' – Patricia de León, actress and former Miss Panama is the latest celebrity to join PETA (People for the Ethical Treatment of Animals), in their condemnation of bullfighting.

ACTIVITY: Protest through poetry

ATL

- Communication skills: Read critically and for comprehension
- Creative-thinking skills: Create original works and ideas; Use existing works and ideas in new ways

'Bloodsports' such as badger baiting were prevalent during the nineteenth century when poet John Clare was writing. Much of his work celebrates rural life and expresses his contempt for the destruction of the countryside, which was a consequence of the Industrial Revolution.

You can learn more about the Industrial Revolution and the impact it had on the countryside by visiting the following website: www.britishmuseum.org/research/publications/online_research_catalogues/paper_money/paper_money_of_england__wales/the_industrial_revolution.aspx

Task 1

Read the poem 'The Badger' on page 115, by John Clare, and then complete the following:

1 **Interpret** the message of the poem.
2 **Analyse** the use of verbs in the poem used to describe:
   a the actions of the people
   b the actions and behaviour of the animals.
3 **Identify** the language Clare uses to present the badger.
4 **Evaluate** how effectively Clare evokes the cruelty of the sport through the language.

Task 2

Use the poem to write a newspaper article about the hunt.

Use the box *How to write a newspaper report* on page 115 to help you.

■ 'Bloodsports' such as badger baiting were popular in the nineteenth century

■ John Clare

The Badger

WHEN midnight comes a host of dogs and men
Go out and track the badger to his den,
And put a sack within the hole and lie
Till the old grunting badger passes by.
He comes and hears – they let the strongest loose.
The old fox hears the noise and drops the goose.
The poacher shoots and hurries from the cry,
And the old hare half wounded buzzes by.
They get a forkéd stick to bear him down
And clap the dogs and take him to the town,
And bait him all the day with many dogs,
And laugh and shout and fright the scampering hogs.
He runs along and bites at all he meets:
They shout and hollo down the noisy streets.

He turns about to face the loud uproar
And drives the rebels to their very door.
The frequent stone is hurled wher'er they go;
When badgers fight, then everyone's a foe.
The dogs are clapped and urged to join the fray;
The badger turns and drives them all away.
Though scarcely half as big, demure and small,
He fights with dogs for hours and beats them all.
The heavy mastiff, savage in the fray,
Lies down and licks his feet and turns away.
The bulldog knows his match and waxes cold
The badger grins and never leaves his hold.
He drives the crowd and follows at their heels
And bites them through – the drunkard swears and reels.

The frighted women take the boys away,
The blackguard laughs and hurries on the fray.
He tries to reach the woods, an awkward race,
But sticks and cudgels quickly stop the chase.
He turns again and drives the noisy crowd
And beats the many dogs in noises loud.
He drives away and beats them every one,
And then they loose them all and set them on.
He falls as dead and kicked by boys and men,
Then starts and grins and drives the crowd again;
Till kicked and torn and beaten out he lies
And leaves his hold and cackles, groans and dies.

By John Clare

How to write a newspaper report

Newspaper reports are a great way of transmitting information in a clear and (usually) objective manner. Follow the guidelines below to help you write your own report:

1   Come up with a suitable headline. This must be catchy, accurate and written in the present tense.

2   Open with with a short and dramatic sentence to hold your reader's attention.

3   Your opening paragraph should provide a brief summary of the event or incident you are reporting.

4   As you are reporting on events that have already happened, use the past tense. Use the active voice generally, but do use the passive voice to account for details you don't know or don't want to reveal.

5   Focus on the facts – **present** these clearly.

6   Use the 5 Ws to help structure your article: <u>W</u>ho is involved? <u>W</u>hat happened? <u>W</u>hen did it happen? <u>W</u>here did it happen? <u>W</u>hy did it happen?

7   Keep your article brief and simple.

8   Include witness testimonies – what did people who were present have to say about the event?

9   Try not to impose your own opinion on readers. Let them make up their own mind about what you are presenting.

10 You may want to **organize** your article using columns and include a picture with a caption.

Should we stop harmful traditions?

HOW CAN WE PROTECT OTHERS FROM DANGEROUS TRADITIONS?

As members of a global community, it is important for us to be principled and take a stand against traditional practices that compromise the safety and well-being of others. We must raise awareness about these harmful practices and encourage members of our local and global communities to help protect those who are the most vulnerable in society.

It can be daunting to speak out against a tradition that has been practised for decades, sometimes centuries; some of these traditions began before we even came into existence and we must accept that it takes time for people to change their point of view about things they have always valued and accepted as being an integral part of their culture. So, while we must be courageous and promote fairness, we must also respect that people have certain beliefs and tackle the subject with sensitivity.

Over the years, the collective efforts of campaigners, activists, charity organizations and us, the people, have helped put an end to harmful traditions including some of the ones we have explored so far in this chapter. Together, we *can* and *must* make a difference.

ℹ Did you know that the tradition of 'sati' in India was finally banned in 1829?

Sati was an ancient Hindu funeral custom, practised in India, where a woman was required to burn to death on her husband's funeral pyre. Many women went voluntarily to their deaths, but some women were forced to comply.

Efforts to stop sati date back as far as the sixteenth century. The Mughal emperor Akbar initially banned the practice, but withdrew the ban for fear of offending his Hindu counterparts.

The practice was criticised by Indian campaigners and British settlers alike; but the British didn't intervene immediately as there were concerns that interfering with cultural practices would upset their relationships with the Hindu community.

In 1829 laws were passed banning sati, but this was not enough to stop the practice continuing in many parts of the country.

Today, India continues to take a firm stance against sati.

Do you know of any dangerous traditions that have been banned in your country?

If not, carry out some research.

■ The Indian reformer Rajah Rammohun Roy campaigned against the cruel practice of sati

■ A painting showing a woman jumping into the flames of her husband's funeral pyre

---

ACTIVITY: Fighting FGM

According to UNICEF (the United Nations International Children's Emergency Fund), at least 200 million girls and women alive today, in over 30 countries across the world, have undergone FGM (Female Genital Mutilation).

Once you are aware of what the process involves, these statistics become all the more shocking.

Task 1

Find out more about FGM by visiting one of the following websites:

www.dofeve.org/about-fgm.html

http://forwarduk.org.uk/key-issues/fgm/

www.nspcc.org.uk/preventing-abuse/child-abuse-and-neglect/female-genital-mutilation-fgm/

FGM is a harmful traditional practice, which has been carried out for centuries. FGM happens to girls in adolescence, childhood or even when they are babies. It is often incorrectly believed to be carried out for religious reasons, but there is very little evidence to suggest that any religion condones such a cruel and potentially fatal practice, and in fact the victims come from many different backgrounds.

Thankfully, we have seen a decline in FGM over the past three decades, but there are still an estimated 3 million girls who are at risk of being cut every year.

Many charity organizations, including Amnesty International and the NSPCC (the National Society for the Prevention of Cruelty to Children), run campaigns to raise awareness of FGM.

➤

Task 2

Look at the campaign posters below and then answer the questions in the boxes:

How are the victims of FGM given a voice in this poster?

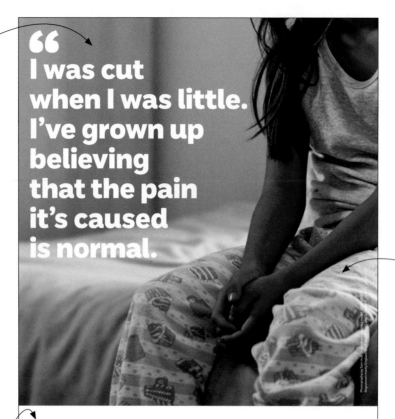

"
I was cut when I was little. I've grown up believing that the pain it's caused is normal.

Female genital mutilation, or 'cutting', is violent, painful and can cause problems that last a lifetime.
It is child abuse and it is illegal.
Every girl has the right to a life free from FGM.

NSPCC

You can help stop it.
For advice and support, call us.
**FGM helpline:
0800 028 3550**
Free. 24/7. Anonymous.
nspcc.org.uk/fgm

EVERY CHILDHOOD IS WORTH FIGHTING FOR

What effect might the image have on the audience?

Identify examples of language used to evoke sympathy for victims of FGM.

Task 3

Visit the website below and on page 119 and watch the videos, and then complete the tasks which follow.

'Needlecraft: an animated story on Female Genital Mutilation'

www.theguardian.com/society/video/2016/may/02/needlecraft-an-animated-story-on-female-genital-mutilation-video

1 **Summarize** the content of the video.
2 **Identify** the possible target audience/s for the video.

3 **Interpret** the message of the video. **Identify** a quote that you think sums up this message.
4 **Analyse** the effect of the music used in the video.
5 Can you infer where the 'story' is set? What do you think the purpose of this is?
6 **Identify** the techniques Needlecraft have used to appeal to a younger audience.
7 Based on what you have learnt so far about FGM in this chapter, can you **understand** why might it be necessary for this video to appeal to a younger audience?
8 Who is responsible for tackling the problem of FGM?

How does the image help support the message of the poster?

Why have Amnesty international included statistics?

Identify examples of language used to encourage people to support the cause.

Every year, two million girls suffer the pain of genital mutilation – a clear violation of their human rights. No government should continue to ignore this crime. Help us to stop violence against women. Give your support at www.amnesty.se

amnesty

'Why did you cut me?'

www.theguardian.com/society/video/2016/feb/05/ mummy-why-did-you-cut-me-survivors-share-pain- fgm-video (Some viewers may find this report distressing.)

1 **Identify** the key difference between this video and the first one.
2 When did Nigeria ban FGM?
3 How long do the effects of FGM last?
4 **Infer** who is involved in imposing this tradition on the young women in the video. How does this make you feel?
5 **Identify** how some of the victims felt while they were being circumcised.

6 What are cited as some of the reasons for carrying out FGM? **Evaluate** why these reasons are problematic?
7 Why are the victims of FGM given a voice in this video? **Interpret** the message they are conveying about tradition.
8 **Evaluate** how effective the two very different videos are.

◆ Assessment opportunities

◆ This activity can be assessed using Criterion B: Comprehending written and visual text.

A brief introduction to essay writing

An essay is a piece of writing through which you can express ideas and arguments about a specific topic. You'll find that that the language you have to use and the conventions you have to follow vary from subject to subject.

Visit this website to read an essay by George Orwell. Don't worry if you don't understand every word: **www.orwell.ru/library/essays/politics/english/e_polit**

1 What is the main argument that Orwell is exploring in his essay?

2 How has he organized his writing?

3 What kind of language does he use? Is it formal or informal? Or somewhere in between?

Let's take a quick look at how an essay should be organized.

> **Hint**
>
> Take care with spelling, punctuation and grammar.
>
> You must use a wide range of vocabulary that is appropriate to the subject in your essay. Do not use contractions such as 'don't'. Apostrophes must be used correctly. Spellings must be correct. There is no excuse for spelling key words incorrectly, such as the names of characters, authors' names and words in the essay question itself.

Essay structure

Introduction

- Plan your ideas, point of view or argument in relation to key themes presented in the essay question.
- Highlight and make use of the key words in the essay question.
- Two or three sentences are sufficient for your introduction.

Main body of the essay

- You must write three to four main paragraphs.
- A substantial paragraph should have four or five sentences or about 100 words.
- Start each paragraph with a topic sentence using the key words (a sentence that explains the main argument of your paragraph).
- Close each paragraph with a link sentence using the key words (a sentence that links your ideas back to the essay question).

Conclusion

- **Summarize** the most significant points that you have discussed in the essay.
- Your essay should be 300–400 words long. Put the word count on the bottom of your final page.
- Font: If you are typing your essay, you should use Times New Roman, size 12 font – this is a standard font, but your school may have a font they prefer, so check.
- Layout: Do not leave more than one line between paragraphs.

ACTIVITY: Is tradition an obstacle to progress?

■ ATL

- Critical-thinking skills: Gather and organize relevant information to formulate an argument; Develop contrary or opposing arguments

1 Read the statement below and ensure that you **understand** what it means.
2 In pairs, **summarize** the statement in one or two sentences.
3 **Evaluate** the statement and decide whether you agree or disagree with the argument that is being presented.

'… it is unacceptable that the international community remains passive (about harmful traditional practices) in the name of a distorted vision of multiculturalism. Human behaviors and cultural values, however senseless or destructive they may appear from the personal and cultural standpoint of others, have meaning and fulfill a function for those who practice them. However, culture is not static but is in constant flux, adapting and reforming. People will change their behavior when they understand the hazards and indignity of harmful practices and when they realize that it is possible to give up harmful practices without giving up meaningful aspects of their culture.' – World Health Organization, 1996

Now, using the statement as a stimulus, plan and write an argumentative essay.

Stuck? Use the 'Tug of war' box opposite and remind yourself how to write to argue by referring to Chapter 5 in *English for the IB MYP 2: by Concept*.

You may need to carry out some research so you have enough material to support your arguments.

◆ Assessment opportunities

- ◆ This activity can be assessed using Criterion C: Communicating in response to spoken and/or written and/or visual text and Criterion D: Using language in spoken and/or written form.

❗ Take action: How can I make a difference?

- ❗ We can all play a part in helping to raise awareness of the plight of people whose lives are affected by the continued practice of harmful traditions.
- ❗ Here are some things you can do:
  - ◆ Raise awareness among your peers by organizing a class debate about whether tradition is an obstacle to progress. Use the box below to help you **organize** your 'tug of war'.
  - ◆ Encourage your school to support a charity that works to eradicate dangerous traditions. Use the internet to carry out some research and then come up with some exciting fundraising ideas.

Tug of war

1 **Present** an argument.
2 **Identify** the factors that 'pull' at each side of the argument. These are the two sides of the tug of war.
3 In groups, think of 'tugs', or reasons why you support a certain side of the argument. Try to think of reasons on the other side of the argument as well.
4 In groups, generate 'what if?' questions to explore the topic further.

SOME SUMMATIVE TASKS TO TRY

Use these tasks to apply and extend your learning in this chapter. These tasks are designed so that you can evaluate your learning at different levels of achievement in the Language acquisition criteria.

Task 1: Writing to argue

'Traditional values are often deployed as an excuse to undermine human rights.'

- Write an essay *for* or *against* the statement above.
- Take some time to plan your essay before writing.
- Make sure you follow the conventions of an *argumentative essay*.
- **Organize** your work into paragraphs.
- Your essay should be 300–400 words long.
- Do not use translating devices or dictionaries for this task.
- You will have 70 minutes to complete this task.

Task 2: Fox hunting

- Visit this website and read the article: **www.league.org.uk/fox-hunting**
- Then answer the following questions, using your own words as much as possible.
- Refer as closely as possible to the story, **justifying** your answers and giving examples when required.
- Do not use translating devices or dictionaries for this task.
- You will have 60 minutes to complete this task.

1 a **Identify** the other types of traditional 'sports' hunting mentioned in the text.   (strand i)
   b What do these 'sports' have in common?   (strand i)
2 How long has fox hunting been around for?   (strand i)
3 **Identify** the origins of fox hunting.   (strand i)
4 What led to it becoming a sporting activity?   (strand i)
5 **Identify** the text type and writer's purpose for writing.   (strand ii)
6 **Infer** why the writer includes facts and statistics.   (strand ii)
7 **Evaluate** how the organization of the text makes it more accessible for readers. (strand ii)
8 **Interpret** the message of the text.   (strand iii)
9 **Analyse** the language used by the writer to create sympathy for the animals.   (strand iii)
10 The writer provides the other side of the argument. **Identify** what this argument is and **infer** why the writer includes it.   (strand i, ii)
11 What kind of effect has this text produced on you as a reader? How do you feel about what you have learnt from the text?   (strand iii)
12 Do you think bans on blood-sports such as fox hunting should be lifted in the UK as they are linked to the country's traditional past? **Explain** why or why not.   (strand iii)

Reflection

In this chapter we have considered what traditions are and have examined why they have become such an integral part of our lives. We have learnt that traditions exist in every **culture** and seen how they can help connect us to our pasts as well as strengthen our bonds with the communities to which we belong. In addition to this we have raised an **argument** about whether or not there is a place for tradition in the modern world and have also explored how some traditions can be harmful and tried to convey a **message** about the need to promote **fairness and development** by giving a **voice** to those most affected.

Use this table to reflect on your own learning in this chapter					
Questions we asked	Answers we found	Any further questions now?			
Factual: What is a tradition? Do traditions vary from place to place?					
Conceptual: How are traditions created? Why are traditions important? How can traditions help us develop a sense of personal and cultural identity? Can traditions be harmful? Is it OK to compromise the safety of animals for the sake of tradition?					
Debatable: Should we stop harmful traditions? How can we protect others from dangerous traditions? Is tradition an obstacle to progress?					
Approaches to learning you used in this chapter:	Description – what new skills did you learn?	How well did you master the skills?			
		Novice	Learner	Practitioner	Expert
Communication skills					
Collaboration skills					
Information literacy skills					
Media literacy skills					
Critical-thinking skills					
Creative-thinking skills					
Learner profile attribute(s)	Reflect on the importance of being principled for your learning in this chapter.				
Principled					

6 How do you see the world?

○ **Scientific and technical innovation** has allowed us to understand how our brain function enables us to learn through **communication**, to **empathise** with others, and to understand how their **way of seeing the world** may differ from our own.

■ We all see the world in different ways

CONSIDER THESE QUESTIONS:

Factual: How do our brains work? What is autism? What is an invisible disability?

Conceptual: Why do we see the world in different ways? How can science and technology help us to understand our brains better? How can literature and art help us to understand others better? How can we practice empathy? How have our attitudes to mental illness changed over time?

Debatable: Why is the number of young people with mental health issues higher than ever before? How can we ensure our mental well-being?

Now **share and compare** your thoughts and ideas with your partner, or with the whole class.

┌○ IN THIS CHAPTER, WE WILL …

■ **Find out** about how our brains work and learn about the different ways in which people perceive the world.

■ **Explore** why we perceive things differently and how we can develop empathy through our exposure to literature and art.

■ **Take action** to raise awareness of neurodiversity and invisible disabilities.

◆ Assessment opportunities in this chapter:

◆ **Criterion A:** Comprehending spoken and visual text

◆ **Criterion B:** Comprehending written and visual text

◆ **Criterion C:** Communicating in response to spoken and/or written and/or visual text

◆ **Criterion D:** Using language in spoken and/or written form

● We will reflect on this learner profile attribute …

● Knowledgeable – we develop and use conceptual understanding, exploring knowledge across a range of disciplines. We engage with issues and ideas that have local and global significance.

These Approaches to Learning (ATL) skills will be useful …

- Communication skills
- Collaboration skills
- Organization skills
- Affective skills

- Reflection skills
- Information literacy skills
- Critical-thinking skills
- Creative-thinking skills

KEY WORDS

autism
invisible disability
neurodiversity
perception

STARTER ACTIVITY

■ ATL

- Creative-thinking skills: Make guesses, ask 'what if' questions and generate testable hypotheses

In pairs, look at the pictures below and **discuss** the questions.

1 What do you think this device was used for?

2 Did this brain belong to a man or a woman? How can you tell?

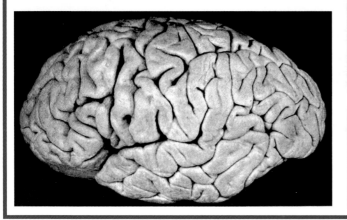

3 Was this person good or bad during their lifetime? Can you guess their profession? (For a clue, look back at page 103 in Chapter 5 of *English for the IB MYP 2: by Concept*.)

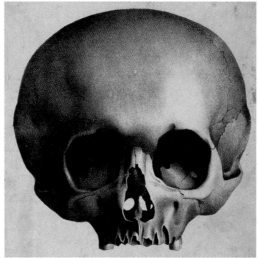

4 What do you think happened to this person?

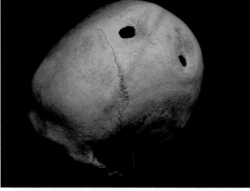

◆ Assessment opportunities

- This activity can be assessed using Criterion C: Communicating in response to spoken and/or written and/or visual text.

How do you see the world?

Most of us move through life with the assumption that the people around us generally see things in the same way as we do. We assume that most people see the same colours as us, understand that there are certain, potentially dangerous situations that should be avoided and interpret the behaviour of others in the same way that we do. We don't stop to consider that perhaps not everyone perceives things exactly as we do.

So, what exactly does it mean to perceive? What is perception? Perception is the way in which we use our senses – sight, hearing, smell, touch and taste – to experience the world around us. But it is more than just this; perception is also how we regard, understand and interpret the things that surround us in our everyday lives, and as we are all different, with different brains and life experiences, then surely our perception and point of view about the world should also vary.

In this chapter we will explore the workings of the human brain and develop a better understanding of the minds of others whose lives and experience of the world may differ considerably from our own.

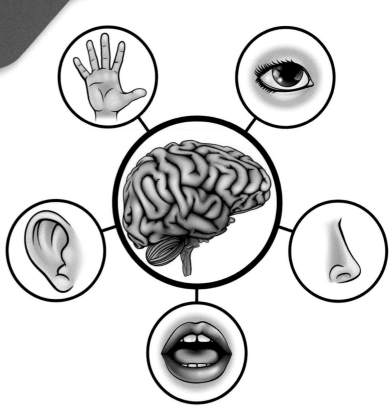

■ We experience the world through our senses

ACTIVITY: The brain – how much do we really know?

■ **ATL**

- Collaborations skills: Delegate and share responsibility for decision-making
- Reflection skills: Consider content

Take another look at the images from the task you completed on page 125.

In pairs, match the images to these descriptions:

a **An illustration that supposedly demonstrates the theory that good or bad character can be related to the shape and size of the skull.**

b **A device for measuring the size of the human heads (and hence brains) of people from different places and of different ethnic minorities. It was developed by**

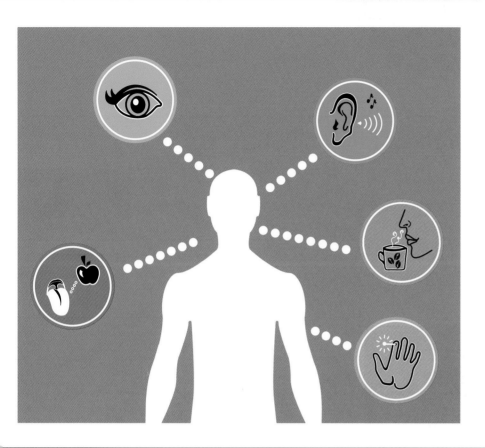

Sir Francis Galton (1822–1911), who believed that there was a link between a person's physical appearance and their intelligence.

c The brain of Helen Hamilton Gardner (1853–1925), a leading American campaigner for women's rights. She challenged contemporary ideas about the differences between the brains of men and women. She argued that the female brain was not 'demonstrably different from that of a man under the same conditions and with the same opportunities for development'.

d A skull of a patient who has undergone trepanation, or trepanning, a process which involves making a hole in the skull through to the surface of the brain. It was used to treat a range of conditions. Some believed that it could help to release evil spirits responsible for causing illness.

Now, reflect on how you feel after reading the descriptions.

1 What do these images tell you about our understanding of the human brain in the past?

2 Have things changed? Do we have a better understanding of how the human brain works?

3 Reflect on what you already know about the brain and write it down. Now write down any questions you have about the brain or about the way in which we see the world. Keep these safe – we will come back to them later.

◆ Assessment opportunities

◆ This activity can be assessed using Criterion B: Comprehending written and visual text.

How do our brains work?

HOW CAN SCIENCE AND TECHNOLOGY HELP US TO UNDERSTAND OUR BRAINS BETTER?

'Everything we do, every thought we've ever had, is produced by the human brain. But exactly how it operates remains one of the biggest unsolved mysteries, and it seems the more we probe its secrets, the more surprises we find.' – Neil deGrasse Tyson

■ Scientist Neil deGrasse Tyson

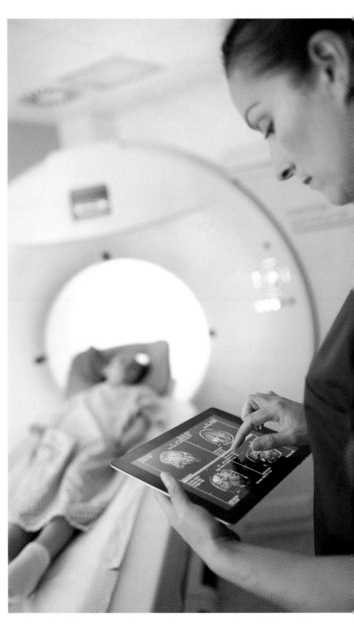

■ Despite the tremendous advancements made in science and technology, the inner workings of the human mind still remain a mystery

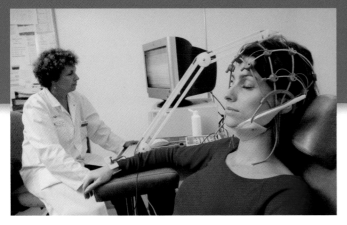

■ Innovations in science and technology have given us a better understanding of the human mind

Think back to the tasks you completed at the beginning of the chapter. How did those images make you feel? Well, rest assured that we have come a long way since the days when measuring skulls and drilling unnecessary holes in people's head were considered appropriate 'scientific' practices.

You will be relieved to know that today, thanks to advancements made in science and technology, we know more about the human brain than ever before. However, as Tyson says, 'exactly how it operates remains one of the biggest unsolved mysteries'.

Scientists worldwide are rising to that challenge of solving these mysteries and the human brain is currently the focus of several (costly) scientific research projects, including the China Brain Project, the EU's Human Brain Project and the US's BRAIN Initiative. You can find out more about these projects by visiting these websites:

www.cell.com/neuron/pdf/S0896-6273(16)30800-5.pdf

www.humanbrainproject.eu

https://braininitiative.nih. gov/?AspxAutoDetectCookieSupport=1

Can you find any more research projects? Perhaps there are some taking place in your home country? Use an internet search engine to find out more.

These projects delve into previously unknown areas to uncover how the brain does what it does but more importantly so that we are able to make progress against the brain disorders that afflict so many people worldwide.

ACTIVITY: What if we could look inside our brains?

■ ATL

■ Communication skills: Make inferences and draw conclusions
■ Organization skills: Use appropriate strategies for organizing complex information

The first steps to unlocking the secrets of our mind is to map the brain. We need to know where everything is. But this is not enough and we still don't fully understand what is happening in our brains – or why – or how. To develop a deeper understanding, we would need to take a look inside …

Visit the following website to watch the video, and then complete the tasks below: http://ed.ted. com/lessons/what-if-we-could-look-inside-human-brains-moran-cerf

1 What is the brain the centre of?
2 **Identify** the two techniques that scientists have used for decades to understand the brain. How do these work? **Infer** what the limitations of these techniques are.
3 What is epilepsy? Write down what you understand.
4 **Identify** and **analyse** the **simile** used to describe epilepsy.
5 How can we look inside the brain? **Summarize** the process in your own words.
6 Why is the brain such a remarkable organ? **List** the reasons mentioned in the video.

◆ Assessment opportunities

◆ This activity can be assessed using Criterion A: Comprehending spoken and visual text.

Links to: Science – Biology

Has what you've covered in this chapter sparked your interest in the workings of the brain? Do you want to find out more about the science behind it? Well, now you can.

Visit this website and **explore** the Science Museum's detailed guide to the brain: **www.sciencemuseum.org.uk/whoami/findoutmore/yourbrain**

Consider the most effective ways of recording what you have learnt, for example, you might want to take detailed notes, or **organize** the information in a table you've created. Work with a partner and see what you come up with.

THINK–PAIR–SHARE

ATL

■ Communication skills: Negotiate ideas and knowledge with peers and teachers

On your own, write down the answers to the following questions. Take some time to think carefully about your responses.

1 **As we continue to make advancements in science and technology and learn more about the way in which the brain works, what do you think we will be able to do with this new knowledge?**
2 **Do you think there is such a thing as a 'normal' brain?**

Now, get into pairs and share your answers.

◆ Assessment opportunities

◆ This activity can be assessed using Criterion C: Communicating in response to spoken and/or written and/or visual text and Criterion D: Using language in spoken and/or written form.

Juxtaposition

Look at the following quote. What contrasts can you find?

'Whatever our souls are made of, his and mine are the same, and Linton's is as different as a moonbeam from lightning, or frost from fire.'

The writer, in this case English poet and novelist Emily Brontë, has drawn contrasts between the following:
- a moonbeam/lightning
- frost/fire

In pairs, consider the connotations of each word and how they differ. How is a moonbeam different from lightning? How does frost differ from fire?

The character who speaks these words in Brontë's novel is comparing two men – Heathcliff (lightning; fire) and Edgar Linton (a moonbeam; frost). What effect does the writer achieve by placing these contrasts together? What do these contrasts reveal about the characters of the two men?

This literary technique, the placing of different words, ideas or elements side by side, is known as **juxtaposition**. Juxtaposition is used to emphasize differences, reveal similarities or explore the relationship between the two contrasting concepts. As readers, we are forced to consider two distinctly different things together.

English for the IB MYP 3: *by Concept*

ACTIVITY: The Monster of Lake LaMetrie

■ An elasmosaurus

A transplant is a complex surgical procedure in which a body tissue or organ is transferred from a donor to a recipient, or from one part of the body to another. So far, a brain transplant has never been conducted. This is because for a transplant of this kind to be successful it would be necessary to connect the nerve fibres from the transplanted brain to the spinal cord of the recipient, which is incredibly difficult.

Task 1

Do you think in the distant future we will be able to carry out brain transplants? Think back to what you have learnt about the brain and **explain** what you think the consequences of a brain transplant could be. In pairs, **discuss** the following:

● **What would this mean in terms of identity? Would the identity of the recipient change? Would they take on characteristics of the donor of their new brain?**
● **Would brain transplants allow us to live for longer?**
● **What moral issues could arise from carrying out a procedure like this?**

Written in 1899, by American science fiction writer Wardon Allan Curtis, 'The Monster of Lake LaMetrie' is a curious short story in which a rather bizarre brain transplant is conducted by the narrator James McLennegan.

In the story, McLennegan, a scientist, and his young companion Edward Framingham discover a living prehistoric reptile in Lake LaMetrie. The men seriously wound the menacing elasmosaurus, and on examination, McLennegan learns that its brain is remarkably similar to that of a human brain. When Framingham dies, McLennegan decides to carry out an experiment using the brain of his friend.

Task 2

On your own, read the extract from the short story on page 132, which begins just after poor Framingham's death, and then complete the following tasks:

1 **Identify** an example of onomatopoeia in the first paragraph.
2 At what point in the extract does the idea to carry out the transplant cross the narrator's mind? What triggers the idea? Find evidence from the text to support your answer.
3 **Identify** and **analyse** the effect of the juxtaposition in the first paragraph.
4 How is the procedure carried out? Consider the writer's use of verbs.
5 Use what the narrator describes in the fourth and fifth paragraphs to **infer** what obstacles prevented brain transplants being carried out.
6 **Interpret** the narrator's views about crime and punishment.
7 What IB learner profile characteristics does the narrator possess? Which does he lack? Find examples from the text to support your answer.

Task 3

In pairs, **discuss** the following:

● **Evaluate** whether there is there anything problematic or immoral about the narrator's experiment? What could the consequences of his experiment be?
● How do you feel about his actions in the extract? Are his decisions justified as being for the sake of scientific progress?

'If you hear me, wink,' I cried. The right eye closed and opened with a snap. Ah, here the body was dead and the brain had lived. I glanced at the elasmosaurus. Its mouth, half closed over its gleaming teeth, seemed to smile an invitation. The intelligence of the man and the strength of the beasts. The living body and the living brain. The curious resemblance of the reptile's brain-pan to that of a man flashed across my mind.

'Are you still alive, Framingham?'

The right eye winked, I seized my machete, for this was no time for delicate instruments. I might destroy all by haste and roughness, I was sure to destroy all by delay. I opened the skull and disclosed the brain. I had not injured it, and breaking the wound of the elasmosaurus's head, placed the brain within, I dressed the wound and, hurrying to the house, brought all my store of stimulants and administered them.

For years the medical fraternity has been predicting that brain grafting will some time be successfully accomplished. Why has it never been successfully accomplished? Because it has not been tried. Obviously, a brain from a dead body cannot be used and what living man would submit to the horrible process of having his head opened, and portions of his brain taken for the use of others?

The brains of men are frequently examined when injured and parts of the brain removed, but parts of the brains of other men have never been substituted for the parts removed. No injured man has even been found who would give any portion of his brain for the use of another.

Until criminals under the sentence of death are handed over to science for experimentation, we shall not know what can be done in the way of brain-grafting. But the public opinion would never allow it.

Conditions are favourable for a fair and thorough trial of my experiment. The weather is cool and even, and the wound in the head of the elasmosaurus has every chance of healing. The animal possesses a vitality superior to any of our later-day animals, and if any organism can successfully become the host of a foreign brain, nourishing it and cherishing it, the elasmosaurus with its abundant vital sources can do it. It may be that a new era in the history of the world will begin here.

Extract from 'The Monster of Lake LaMetrie', by Wardon Allan Curtis

Why do we see the world in different ways?

WHAT IS AUTISM?

We all see, or rather perceive, the world in different ways. So far we have established that this is because of the differences in the way that our brains work. In the past, we have often looked upon these 'neurological' differences as deviating from what society thinks is 'normal'. But there is no such thing as 'normal' and it becomes problematic when we use the same measure to define and label everyone. As IB learners, we strive to celebrate differences of all kinds – ethnic, religious, cultural – so why shouldn't this extend to neurological differences?

Neurodiversity is the word we use to describe these differences and, as a society, we must recognize and respect the fact that we don't all perceive the world in the same way. For some of us, particularly if we have, for example, dyspraxia, dyslexia, ADHD (attention deficit hyperactivity disorder) or autism, perceiving and interpreting the world around us can be less straightforward than it is for the majority of people. Seeing these as examples of neurodiversity rather than 'diseases' that need to be cured, is more positive for all of us.

> ### EXTENSION
>
> Don't know what dyspraxia, dyslexia or ADHD are? Use a search engine to find out more.

In this section we will look more at neurodiversity and develop a better understanding of people who are neurologically different from ourselves.

ACTIVITY: What is autism?

■ ATL

- Communication skills: Make inferences and draw conclusions

Founded in 1962, the National Autistic Society (NAS) is a British charity dedicated to improving the lives of people with autistic spectrum disorders. For the past five decades they have worked hard to raise awareness and understanding of autism and Asperger syndrome.

Visit the following website to watch a video and then complete the tasks below: **www.youtube.com/watch?v=d4G0HTIUBII**

1   **What is the purpose of the video?**
2   **Approximately how many people in the UK have autism?**
3   **What is autism?**
4   **What can be confusing for autistic people to understand?**
5   **What do you understand by 'spectrum condition', based on the explanation provided in the video?**
6   **All autistic people experience the same thing. Is this true or false? Find evidence to support your answer.**
7   **Despite being of average or above average intelligence, what do people with Asperger syndrome sometimes have difficulties with?**
8   **What is autism like? Make notes about what you learn.**
9   **What characteristics do people with autism often possess?**

◆ Assessment opportunities

- ◆ This activity can be assessed using Criterion A: Comprehending spoken and visual text.

ACTIVITY: Raising awareness

■ **ATL**

- ■ Collaboration skills: Practise empathy
- ■ Communication skills: Make inferences and draw conclusions

Look at the two posters below and on page 135 and then complete the following tasks:

1 What purpose do the posters share?
2 Who is the target audience for each poster? Make sure you can **justify** your answer.
3 For each poster, **interpret** the specific message the creators are trying to convey.

4 How do the charities create empathy for people with autism? **Evaluate** which of the two posters best illustrates the experience of being an autistic child.
5 For each poster, **identify** and **analyse** the language and visual clues the creator has used to get their message across.
6 **Identify** which poster has used an idiom to show just how little we understand about autistic behavior. What is this idiom? **Interpret** what it means. Use the internet to help you if you get stuck.

◆ Assessment opportunities

◆ This activity can be assessed using Criterion B: Comprehending written and visual text.

Autism: understanding behaviour

Caroline Hattersley

The National Autistic Society

What is an invisible disability?

While almost everyone has an understanding of what a disability is, many people fail to realize that not all disabilities can be *seen*. Some disabilities are more obvious than others; for example, someone with a disability that limits their mobility may be recognizable by a wheelchair or walking frame.

Invisible disabilities – ones that cannot be seen by the naked eye – are not immediately apparent and as a result aren't always treated with the attention, sensitivity or respect that they deserve. Although some invisible or hidden disabilities, such as mental illness and learning difficulties, may not be physically inhibiting, they can have an incredibly debilitating effect on the day-to-day lives of people who have them.

ACTIVITY: What is mental health?

ATL

- Collaboration skills: Practise empathy
- Creative-thinking skills: Use brainstorming and visual diagrams to generate new ideas and inquiries
- Information literacy skills: Evaluate and select information sources and digital tools based on their appropriateness to specific tasks
- Communication skills: Use appropriate forms of writing for different purposes and audiences

Task 1

In pairs, **create** two mind maps of everything you understand about the following:

MENTAL HEALTH

MENTAL ILLNESS

Task 2

Discuss the following questions:

1 Use an internet search engine and type in mental health statistics to find out how many people are affected or likely to be affected by mental health issues during their lifetime. You can do this for your own country, where you are living now, or worldwide.
2 Reflect on the statistics you have found. Do these figures surprise you? **Explain** why.
3 What ordinary life events do you find stressful? For example, consider exams or speaking in public. Do you think most people would find these things stressful? How would these things be worse for people who suffer from mental health issues?
4 How do long-term illnesses – physical or mental – affect people's day-to-day lives? What impact might an illness have on the person who is suffering from it? What about the people around them, such as friends and family?

5 Is it easier to discuss physical illness than mental illness? Why do you think this is? What does this reveal about society's attitude towards mental illness?

6 How are people who suffer from mental illness presented in the media? What is your opinion of this?

Task 3

Use the internet to find some websites you can use to carry out some research about one of the following mental health issues:

- depression
- bipolar disorder
- body dysmorphic disorder (BDD)
- obsessive-compulsive disorder (OCD)
- anxiety and panic attacks.

Collate a list of the websites you have found and **evaluate** them to ensure that you only use reliable sources of information.

Find out as much as you can about your selected mental health issue, including how it affects the lives of teenagers.

Task 4

Use the information you have gathered to **create** a leaflet or brochure about your selected mental health issue. The target audience for your leaflet should be young people of your age group, so think carefully about your choice of language.

◆ Assessment opportunities

- ◆ This activity can be assessed using Criterion C: Communicating in response to spoken and/or written and/or visual text and Criterion D: Using language in spoken and/or written form.

So far in this chapter we have learnt that through scientific and technical innovation we now have a better understanding of how the brain works than ever before. We have been introduced to the concept of neurodiversity and understand that we all perceive the world in different ways and that this diversity should be recognized and respected by all.

How can literature and art help us to understand others better?

HOW CAN WE PRACTISE EMPATHY?

In their work, artists and writers often show empathy for what society has been quick to label as 'illness', 'disease' or 'abnormality', and through viewing these paintings and reading these poems and stories, we can enhance our understanding of mental illness and learning differences. Art and literature can teach us to stop seeing invisible disabilities as something alien and can encourage us to speak openly about these issues which affect the lives of millions of people around the world.

Not only can literature and art reveal how invisible disabilities are (today) and were (in the past) understood and treated, but they can also help us to manage our feelings when we ourselves are struggling to make sense of the world, whether that be through considering the work of others or producing our own. Take for instance, art therapy, a form of psychotherapy that uses art to address emotional issues, which may be confusing and distressing for people who are experiencing them.

In this section we will look at examples of literature that may help us to understand others better and how paintings, poems and stories can challenge the bias towards invisible disabilities that we so frequently encounter in our society.

ACTIVITY: The Curious Incident of the Dog in the Night-Time

■ ATL

- Communication skills: Read critically and for comprehension
- Creative-thinking skills: Make unexpected or unusual connections between objects and/or ideas

The Curious Incident of the Dog in the Night-Time is a novel set in England about a teenage boy called Christopher, who has an invisible disability, and who discovers a murdered poodle on a neighbour's lawn. The book has been a huge success with children and adults alike and millions of copies have been sold worldwide.

The novel's author, Mark Haddon, is very keen not to label the book as being 'about Asperger's'. Instead, he says that it should be seen as 'a novel about difference, about being an outsider, about seeing the world in a surprising and revealing way. It's as much a novel about us as it is about Christopher.'

In pairs, **discuss** the following:

- **What do you think the author means when he says 'It's as much a novel about us as it is about Christopher'? What do you think we learn about our own point of view about difference when we read the novel?**
- **Why do you think he is reluctant to label Christopher as having Asperger syndrome?**

Read the extract on pages 139–141 and consider the following questions:

1 **Identify** the narrative voice used in the novel.
2 **Analyse** the effect it has on the audience.
3 Think back to the National Autistic Society (NAS) video you watched earlier. **Synthesize** what you have learnt about autism and Asperger syndrome and see if you can make any connections with Christopher's point of view, behaviour or experiences with others. Find examples from the text to support your response.
4 How does the extract allow you to empathize with Christopher?
5 Which IB learner profile characteristics does Christopher possess? Find quotes from the text to support your answer.

◆ Assessment opportunities

◆ This activity can be assessed using Criterion B: Comprehending written and visual text and Criterion C: Communicating in response to spoken and/or written and/or visual text.

This is a murder mystery novel.

Siobhan said that I should write something I would want to read myself. Mostly I read books about science and maths. I do not like proper novels. In proper novels people say things like, 'I am veined with iron, with silver and with streaks of common mud. I cannot contract into the firm fist which those clench who do not depend on stimulus'[1]. What does this mean? I do not know. Nor does Father. Nor do Siobhan or Mr Jeavons. I have asked them.

Siobhan has long blonde hair and wears glasses which are made of green plastic. And Mr Jeavons smells of soap and wears brown shoes that have approximately 60 tiny circular holes in each of them.

But I do like murder mystery novels. So I am writing a murder mystery novel.

In a murder mystery novel someone has to work out who the murderer is and then catch them. It is a puzzle. If it is a good puzzle you can sometimes work out the answer before the end of the book.

Siobhan said that the book should begin with something to grab people's attention. That is why I started with the dog. I also started with the dog because it happened to me and I find it hard to imagine things which did not happen to me.

Siobhan read the first page and said that it was different. She put this word into inverted commas by making the wiggly quotation sign with her first and second fingers. She said that it was usually people who were killed in murder mystery novels. I said that two dogs were killed in *The Hound of the Baskervilles*, the hound itself and James Mortimer's spaniel, but Siobhan said they weren't the victims of the murder, Sir Charles Baskerville was. She said that this was because readers cared more about people than dogs, so if a person was killed in the book readers would want to carry on reading.

I said that I wanted to write about something real and I knew people who had died but I did not know any people who had been killed, except Edward's father from school, Mr Paulson, and that was a gliding accident, not murder, and I didn't really know him. I also said that I cared about dogs because they were faithful and honest, and some dogs were cleverer and more interesting than some people. Steve, for example, who comes to school on Thursdays, needs help to eat his food and could not even fetch a stick. Siobhan asked me not to say this to Steve's mother.

…

1. I found this in a book when Mother took me into the library in town in 1996

Then the police arrived. I like the police. They have uniforms and numbers and you know what they are meant to be doing. There was a policewoman and a policeman. The policewoman had a little hole in her tights on her left ankle and a red scratch in the middle of the hole. The policeman had a big orange leaf stuck to the bottom of his shoe which was poking out from one side.

The policewoman put her arms round Mrs Shears and led her back towards the house.

I lifted my head off the grass.

The policeman squatted down beside me and said, 'Would you like to tell me what's going on here, young man?'.

I sat up and said 'The dog is dead.'

'I'd got that far,' he said.

I said, 'I think someone killed the dog.'

'How old are you?' he asked.

I replied, 'I am 15 years and 3 months and 2 days.'

'And what, precisely, were you doing in the garden?' he asked.

'I was holding the dog,' I replied.

'And why were you holding the dog?' he asked.

This was a difficult question. It was something I wanted to do. I like dogs. It made me sad to see that the dog was dead.

I like policemen, too, and I wanted to answer the question properly, but the policeman did not give me enough time to work out the correct answer.

'Why were you holding the dog?' he asked again.

'I like dogs,' I said.

'Did you kill the dog?' he asked.

I said, 'I did not kill the dog.'

'Is this your fork?' he asked.

I said, 'No.'

'You seem very upset about this,' he said.

He was asking too many questions and he was asking them too quickly. They were stacking up in my head like loaves in the factory where Uncle Terry works. The factory is a bakery and he operates the slicing machines. And sometimes the slicer is not working fast enough but the bread keeps coming and there is a blockage. I sometimes think of my mind as a machine, but not always as a bread-slicing machine. It makes it easier to explain to other people what is going on inside it.

The policeman said, 'I am going to ask you once again...'

I rolled back onto the lawn and pressed my forehead to the ground again and made the noise that Father calls groaning. I make this noise when there is too much information coming into my head from the outside world. It is like when you are upset and you hold the radio against your ear and you tune it halfway between two stations so that all you get is white noise and then you turn the volume right up so that this is all you can hear and then you know you are safe because you cannot hear anything else.

The policeman took hold of my arm and lifted me onto my feet.

I didn't like him touching me like this.

And this is when I hit him.

...

This will not be a funny book. I cannot tell jokes because I do not understand them. Here is a joke, as an example. It is one of Father's.

His face was drawn but the curtains were real.

I know why this is meant to be funny. I asked. It is because *drawn* has three meanings, and they are **1)** drawn with a pencil, **2)** exhausted, and **3)** pulled across a window, and meaning **1** refers to both the face and the curtains, meaning **2** refers only to the face, and meaning **3** refers only to the curtains.

If I try to say the joke to myself, making the word mean the three different things at the same time, it is like hearing three different pieces of music at the same time which is uncomfortable and confusing and not nice like white noise. It is like three people trying to talk to you at the same time about different things.

And that is why there are no jokes in this book.

Extract from The Curious Incident of the Dog in the Night-Time, *by Mark Haddon*

ACTIVITY: Depression and the power of words

■ ATL

■ Information literacy skills: Access information to be informed and inform others
■ Critical-thinking skills: Draw reasonable conclusions and generalizations
■ Communication skills: Read critically and for comprehension

Do words have the power to help people cope with mental illness?

Visit the websites below to read about how poetry can help people in their darkest moments:

www.mind.org.uk/information-support/your-stories/depression-and-the-power-of-words/#.WJtpIGMy7zJ

www.telegraph.co.uk/culture/books/10820048/Rachel-Kelly-How-poetry-helped-me-recover-from-depression.html

In pairs, **discuss** the question above and what you have just read, and consider why and how literature can produce this kind of effect.

Now read the two poems opposite and then complete the following tasks:

1 Use an internet search engine to find out about when the poems were written and why. Consider the obstacles the two men were up against. One of the poets is thought to have been depressed.
2 **Evaluate** the poems and decide which one:
    a gives you the best insight into depression
    b could be used to help someone through their depression.
3 Bearing in mind your response to Question 2, **identify** and **analyse** the language and stylistic choices made by the writers to convey their point of view. Consider how the writers create empathy.
4 Which poem do you like most? **Discuss** this with a partner and make sure you can **justify** your choice.
5 What connections can you make between the poems and the two online articles?

◆ Assessment opportunities

◆ This activity can be assessed using Criterion B: Comprehending written and visual text and Criterion C: Communicating in response to spoken and/or written and/or visual text.

Alone

From childhood's hour I have not been
As others were – I have not seen
As others saw – I could not bring
My passions from a common spring –
From the same source I have not taken
My sorrow – I could not awaken
My heart to joy at the same tone –
And all I lov'd – *I* lov'd alone –
Then – in my childhood – in the dawn
Of a most stormy life – was drawn
From ev'ry depth of good and ill
The mystery which binds me still –
From the torrent, or the fountain –
From the red cliff of the mountain –
From the sun that 'round me roll'd
In its autumn tint of gold –
From the lightning in the sky
As it pass'd me flying by –
From the thunder, and the storm –
And the cloud that took the form
(When the rest of Heaven was blue)
Of a demon in my view –

By Edgar Allan Poe

Invictus

Out of the night that covers me,
　　Black as the Pit from pole to pole,
I thank whatever gods may be
　　For my unconquerable soul.

In the fell clutch of circumstance
　　I have not winced nor cried aloud.
Under the bludgeonings of chance
　　My head is bloody, but unbowed.

Beyond this place of wrath and tears
　　Looms but the Horror of the shade,
And yet the menace of the years
　　Finds, and shall find, me unafraid.

It matters not how strait the gate,
　　How charged with punishments the
　　scroll.
I am the master of my fate:
　　I am the captain of my soul.

By William Ernest Henley

Did you know that many of the world's most important artists and writers suffered from mental health issues?

Samuel Johnson, Virginia Woolf, Sylvia Plath, Edvard Munch, Ernest Hemingway and Vincent Van Gogh were all affected by mental illness during their lifetimes.

The painting below, entitled 'Portrait of a Young Man', was painted by the artist Richard Dadd in 1853.

■ 'Portrait of a Young Man'

In pairs, **discuss** your first impressions of the painting. Who is the man in the picture? Where might it be set?

The portrait was painted in the grounds of Bethlehem Royal Hospital, an institution for the mentally ill in London – a place you'll learn more about later in this chapter. Richard Dadd became a patient at the hospital after stabbing his father and fleeing the country. While he was at Bethlem (and then later at another hospital, Broadmoor) he was encouraged to continue painting and many of his best-known works were produced during this time.

EXTENSION

Many celebrities have bravely spoken out about their invisible disabilities.

Choose one of the following people and carry out some research about their experiences with mental illness or learning difficulties. Find out how they overcame obstacles and about any strategies they use to manage their condition.

Prepare a presentation for your peers.

■ (Clockwise from top-left) Orlando Bloom, Daniel Radcliffe, Cara Delevingne, Michael Phelps, Selena Gomez, Richard Branson, Whoopi Goldberg

How have our attitudes to mental illness changed over time?

In the past, attitudes towards mental illness were far from positive. People who suffered from mental health issues or those who displayed signs of what we now accept to be neurodiversity, were often misunderstood and marginalized.

The treatment of the mentally ill was often left in the hands of people who weren't sensitive to the needs of patients in their care, and methods of treatment could be cruel and inhumane. People with mental illnesses were considered a burden on their families, a source of shame and embarrassment, and they often found themselves confined in asylums where they were stripped of their dignity and subjected to humiliations which in today's world would not be tolerated.

It was not until the late twentieth century that attitudes began to change, and thankfully in today's world we are more tolerant and understanding of mental health issues than people were in the past. However, we still have a long way to go, and many mindsets to change, before the stigma that is sometimes associated with mental illness is completely eliminated.

■ The Royal Bethlehem Hospital or Bedlam (Londoners started calling the hospital 'Bethlem', an abbreviation of Bethlehem)

■ 'A Rake's Progress' by William Hogarth: Two fashionable ladies visit 'Bedlam' to see the patients

ACTIVITY: Bedlam

The Royal Bethlehem Hospital, or Bedlam as it is commonly known, is considered to be the world's oldest psychiatric institution. Founded in 1247, the original hospital was located in the City of London and was set up to specialize in the care of the mentally ill. Since then, it has moved three times and the current hospital is based in Beckenham, south London, where it has provided quality care to patients since the 1930s.

The hospital's nickname, 'Bedlam', has become synonymous with chaos and disorder and although it is a reputable institution now, things haven't always been this way. Let's find out more.

Task 1

Go to this website and follow the instructions below: http://learning.museumofthemind.org.uk/visiting-bethlem/

1 Click on 'Click here to begin'.
2 Click on the 'ATTITUDES TO MENTAL HEALTH' tab in the top left-hand corner of the page. You'll find that you can use your cursor to scroll along the timeline at the bottom of the page, but you'll have plenty of time to explore later.

3 For now, click on the 1676 FAQ to watch the short video.
4 **Summarize** the content of the video.
5 Listen carefully to Dr Andrews and **interpret** what attitudes towards mental health were like in the seventeenth century.
6 In pairs, **discuss** what point of view people in today's world would have about the behaviour and expectations of the visitors described in the video.
7 Take some time to **explore** the rest of the timeline. If you want to learn more about the hospital, click on the other tabs at the top of the page.

Task 2: Bedlam diary

Once you have learnt more about the experiences of the patients at Bedlam in the past, consider how they might have felt. Put yourself in their shoes and **create** a mind map to help you **organize** your ideas.

Write a diary entry from the perspective of a patient at Bedlam during the seventeenth century.

Why is the number of young people with mental health issues higher than ever before?

HOW CAN WE ENSURE OUR MENTAL WELL-BEING?

In the UK alone, rates of depression and anxiety among teenagers have increased by 70 per cent in the past 25 years. These are incredibly worrying statistics and as a society we must investigate why this is the case.

In the past, due to the stigma of mental health and a general lack of awareness, it has been difficult to measure the number of people, particularly teenagers, who suffer from anxiety and depression. However, as we are now better equipped to support those with mental health needs, and with the increasing number of celebrities speaking openly about their own illnesses, it has become easier for teenagers to talk about their experiences. While this open discourse about mental health can only be a positive thing, it doesn't make the statistics any less concerning.

So, why are teenagers feeling so anxious? In this section we will consider some of the factors that may contribute to the rise in mental illness in young people and consider strategies to help reduce stress and anxiety in our day-to-day lives.

THINK–PAIR–SHARE

■ ATL

- Collaboration skills: Practise empathy
- Affective skills: Practise strategies to reduce stress and anxiety
- Communication skills: Use appropriate forms of writing for different purposes and audiences

What affects young people's mental health? On your own, think about all of the pressures young people face in today's world. Jot down your thoughts in a mind map.

Share your mind map with a partner or in a group. Do you see any similarities in the mind maps? Take some time to **discuss** your ideas.

Now, come up with suggestions about how young people can manage these pressures and reduce stress and anxiety.

Use the ideas you have generated during your discussion to write an open letter to young people.

Consider the following to help you plan your letter:

- **Your audience is people your age – will your letter be formal or informal?**
- **What is the purpose of your letter? Is it to inform them about the rise of mental health issues in people of their age group? Is it to advise them on how to cope with stress and anxiety? Is it to persuade them to change they way they think about some of the pressures you discussed earlier? It's entirely up to you.**
- **Once you have identified your purpose, think carefully about the language and stylistic choices you will need to make.**

If you need some more ideas, visit the following website: **www.mentalhealth.org.uk/a-to-z/c/children-and-young-people**

◆ Assessment opportunities

- ◆ This activity can be assessed using Criterion C: Communicating in response to spoken and/or written and/or visual text and Criterion D: Using language in spoken and/or written form.

ACTIVITY: How can we be more sensitive to the needs of others?

■ ATL

- ■ Communication skills: Make inferences and draw conclusions

Although there is now a far greater awareness of mental illnesses such as depression and anxiety, there is still a tendency to treat people with these illnesses differently from those with more obvious, physical illnesses. It is important that we **recognize** that invisible disabilities should be treated with the same sensitivity and respect as other illnesses.

Look at the visual text on page 150, entitled 'What If People Treated Physical Illness Like Mental Illness?', and then complete the following tasks:

1 **Identify** the audience and purpose of the text.
2 **Interpret** the message of the text.
3 **How is this message conveyed both visually and through language?**
4 **How does the creator of the image create empathy for people who have mental illnesses? Evaluate how effective the image is.**
5 **How does the image make you feel? Discuss in pairs or groups.**

◆ Assessment opportunities

- ◆ This activity can be assessed using Criterion B: Comprehending written and visual text and Criterion C: Communicating in response to spoken and/or written and/or visual text.

■ What If People Treated Physical Illness Like Mental Illness?

Take action: Opportunity to apply learning through action …

! **Create** a chill-out hub in your school: Write a letter to your school principal, asking them to create a quiet space where students can go when they're feeling stressed or anxious.

! Raise awareness of invisible disabilities during Mental Health Awareness Week. Find out more about how you can get involved by visiting the following website: **http://mentalhealth.org.uk/ campaigns/mental-health-awareness-week/get-involved**

! Look after your own mental health: Eat well, get plenty of exercise, sleep well and make sure you talk to people around you if you are feeling anxious or depressed. You don't have to deal with things on your own.

A SUMMATIVE TASK TO TRY

Use this task to apply and extend your learning in this chapter. This task is designed so that you can evaluate your learning in the Language acquisition criteria.

THIS TASK CAN BE USED TO EVALUATE YOUR LEARNING IN CRITERION B TO PHASE 6

- Visit this website and look at the poster: **www.goo.gl/yWEHCD**
- Then answer the following questions, using your own words as much as possible.
- Do not use translating devices or dictionaries for this task.
- You will have 70 minutes to complete this task.

1 **Identify** the purpose of the text.   (strand i)
2 Parents are the main target audience for this poster. Is this statement true or false? **Justify** your response with evidence from the poster.   (strand i)
3 **Interpret** the message of the text.   (strand iii)
4 **Identify** an example of juxtaposition in the text.   (strand i)
5 **Analyse** the effect of the juxtaposition on the audience.   (strand ii)
6 How does the poster create empathy for Brianna and her family? **Analyse** the language and visual clues used for this purpose.   (strands ii & iii)
7 **Evaluate** how successfully the poster engages the target audience.   (strand iii)
8 Based on this poster, what problems do you think autistic people and their families in the UK face today? **Explain** your answer in detail with reference to the poster.   (strand iii)
9 How aware are people in your home country of autism spectrum disorders? Do you know of any charities that support people who have autism?   (strand iii)
10 Do you think the poster can help to change the way people think about autism? What could you do to help raise awareness about this cause?   (strand iii)

Reflection

In this chapter we have learnt a little about the complexities of the human brain – something only possible thanks to **scientific and technical innovation**. In addition to this, we have considered how we all perceive the world in different ways and have celebrated this neurodiversity. We have also learnt about invisible disabilities and have challenged our existing **points of view** about mental illness. We have seen how, through exploring literature and art, we can learn **empathy** for others and change the way in which we **communicate** with those who have different learning needs to our own.

Use this table to reflect on your own learning in this chapter					
Questions we asked	Answers we found	Any further questions now?			
Factual: How do our brains work? What is autism? What is an invisible disability?					
Conceptual: Why do we see the world in different ways? How can science and technology help us to understand our brains better? How can literature and art help us to understand others better? How can we practise empathy? How have our attitudes to mental illness changed over time?					
Debatable: Why is the number of young people with mental health issues higher than ever before? How can we ensure our mental well-being?					
Approaches to learning you used in this chapter:	Description – what new skills did you learn?	How well did you master the skills?			
		Novice	Learner	Practitioner	Expert
Communication skills					
Collaboration skills					
Organization skills					
Affective skills					
Reflection skills					
Information literacy skills					
Critical-thinking skills					
Creative-thinking skills					
Learner profile attribute(s)	Reflect on the importance of being knowledgeable for your learning in this chapter.				
Knowledgeable					

Glossary

acrostic A poem or word puzzle in which certain letters in each line spell out a particular word or phrase

accent The way people pronounce words

active voice When the subject of the sentence performs the action of the verb, for example, *Peter broke the window.*

adjective A word that describes a person, place or thing

archaic Very old or old fashioned

Cockney A person who was born and lives in the East End of London, traditionally within the sound of Bow bells. Cockneys have a specific dialect and pronunciation

colloquial language Everyday language and expressions as used in conversation

dialect Words or phrases that you usually hear in a particular geographical area. For example Cockney in the East End of London

docudrama A dramatized television film based on real events

empathy The ability to understand and share the feelings of another person

fictional Invented as part of a work of fiction, which describes imaginary people, events or places

first person narrative voice Told from the viewpoint of the character who is speaking or writing, using first person pronouns such as 'I' and 'we'

genre A style of a book or film

idiom An expression, usually specific to a particular culture or language, which means something different from its literal meaning

imperative Verbs or sentences that are used to give commands or instructions

juxtaposition Placing different words, ideas or elements side by side

metaphorical Not literal, but symbolic; using images

onomatopoeia Words that create or represent sounds

narrative A story or account of events

narrative voice The voice of the person telling the story (see first person narrative voice)

narrator A person who tells the story

noun A person, place, or thing

paragraph A series of sentences grouped together and linked by a common topic; found in prose

passive voice When the subject of the sentence has something done to it by someone or something, for example, *The window was broken by Peter.*

persona A role or character adopted by an author

phrasal verb A verb that consists of a basic verb and another word or words. The two or three words that make up a phrasal verb form a short phrase

pronoun A word that can be used to replace a noun

proper noun The name of a person, place or organization; always begins with a capital letter

protagonist The leading character, hero or heroine in a novel or other literary work

register The style of language used in a specific context

repetition The repetition of words or grammatical structures for emphasis or to create a desired effect

sentence A grammatical structure made with one or more words that can be a statement, question or command

setting The time or place in which a story takes place

simile A way of describing something by comparing it to something else, often using the word 'like' or 'as'

slang Language that is used informally, particularly in speaking

Standard English The style of English language that is considered to be the accepted way to communicate, especially in a formal context

synonym A word that means exactly or nearly the same as another word in the same language

verb A word that expresses an action or a state of being

Acknowledgements

The Publishers would like to thank the following for permission to reproduce copyright material. Every effort has been made to trace all copyright holders, but if any have been inadvertently overlooked the Publishers will be pleased to make the necessary arrangements at the first opportunity.

Photo credits

p.2 *l* ©Tijana87/iStock/Thinkstock, *r* © Sylverarts/iStock/Thinkstock; **p.3** © SIphotography/ iStock/Thinkstock; **p.4** © International Baccalaureate Organization; **p.7** *tl*© Toa55/Shutterstock, *ml* © 2p2play/Shutterstock, *bl* ©Purestock/ iStock/Thinkstock, *tr* © Creatas/iStock/Thinkstock, *mr* © Moodboard/Thinkstock, *br* © WavebreakmediaMicro/Fotolia; **p.8** *l* © cacaroot/iStock/Thinkstock, *r* © Africa Studio/Shutterstock; **p.10** © johan63/iStock/Thinkstock; **p.12** *t* © Ninamalyna/123RF, *b* © Monty Rakusen/Cultura/Getty Images; **p.14** © See Li/Alamy Stock Photo; **p.17** *l* ©Lucian Milasan/Alamy Stock Photo, *r* © Frances Roberts/Alamy Stock Photo; **p.20** *l* © Gustavo Frazao/Shutterstock, *c* © SFerdon/Shutterstock, *r* © Dzmitry Kliapitski/Alamy Stock Photo; **p.21** © Gualtiero boffi/Shutterstock; **p.23** © Feng Yu/Shutterstock; **p.26** *t* © Lakov Filimonov/123RF, *b* © Monkey Business Images/Shutterstock; **p.28** © Alphaspirit/123RF; **p.30** © Matthew Chattle/Alamy Stock Photo; **p.33** © UPP/TopFoto; **p.34** © Kathy deWitt/Alamy Stock Photo; **p.35** © dizanna/123RF; **p.38** *l* © Iakov Filimonov/ Shutterstock, *r* © Inegvin/Shutterstock; **p.40** *t* © Poprotskiy Alexey/Shutterstock, *m* © Look Die Bildagentur der Fotografen GmbH/Dietmar Denger/Alamy Stock Photo, *b* © Andrew wrighting/Alamy Stock Photo; **p.41** © imageBROKER/FB-Fischer/ Alamy Stock Photo; **p.42** © lp studio/Shutterstock; **p.44** © Pixsooz/Shutterstock; **p.45** © RosaIreneBetancourt 7/Alamy Stock Photo; **p.46** *tl* © Library Of Congress, Prints and Photographic Division [LC-USZ61-791], *tr* © Granger, NYC/TopFoto, *b* © Library of Congress, Prints and Photographic Division [LC-DIG-anrc-15235]; **p.48** © Steve estvanik/Shutterstock; **p.55** *t* © ImageBROKER/Alamy Stock Photo, *b* © PCN Photography/Alamy Stock Photo ©; **p.57** © Keystone Pictures USA/Alamy Stock Photo; **p.60** © Balint Roxana/123 RF; **p.61** © Maglara/Shutterstock; **p.62** © LianeM/Shutterstock; **p.63** *t* © Maglara/ Shutterstock , *b* © 135pixels/Shutterstock; **p.66** *t* © WENN Ltd/Alamy Stock Photo , *b* © Photo 12/Alamy Stock Photo; **p.68** © Shandarov Arkadii/Shutterstock; **p.69** *tl* © Raga Jose Fuste/Prisma by Dukas Presseagentur GmbH/Alamy Stock Photo, *tr* © Icreative3d/123RF, *bl* © Hagit Berkovich/123RF, *br* © Sean Pavone/Shutterstock; **p.70** *l* © Library of Congress, *m* © Penguin Books Ltd., 2008. Reproduced by permission of Penguin Random House UK, *r* © llucky78/Shutterstock; **p.72** © Interfoto/Alamy Stock Photo; **p.73** © 19th era/Alamy Stock Photo; **p.74** *l* © Lebrecht Authors/Lebrecht Music and Arts Photo Library/Alamy Stock Photo, *r* © North Wind Picture Archives/Alamy Stock Photo; **p.75** © Granger, NYC/TopFoto; **p.76** © CSU Archives/Everett Collection/Alamy Stock Photo; **p.77** © Mick Sinclair/Alamy Stock Photo; **p.79** *l* © Topfoto, *m* © Peter Horree/Alamy Stock Photo, *r* © Archivart/Alamy Stock Photo; **p.80** © PR Image Factory/Shutterstock; **p.81** © Stephen Frost/Alamy Stock Photo; **p.88** *l* © Sturti/E+/Getty Images, *r* © Yulia Mayorova/Shutterstock; **p.90** *t* © AA World Travel Library/TopFoto, *b* © NH7/Fotolia; **p.92** *t* © EduardSV/Shutterstock , *m* © Wong Sze Yuen/Shutterstock , *b* © Andrew Duke/Alamy Stock Photo; **p.94** © JeniFoto/ Shutterstock; **p.95** *l* © Akiyoko/Shutterstock , *ml* © Prisma by Dukas Presseagentur GmbH/Alamy Stock Photo, *mr* © India Picture/Shutterstock, *r* © Anatoliy Nykilchyk/123RF; **p.96** *t* © Strelok/123RF, *b* © Neha Gupta/Alamy Stock Photo; **p.98** © AP/ Rex/Shutterstock; **p.106** © B Christopher/Alamy Stock Photo; **p.107** © Library Of Congress, Prints and Photographic Division [LC-USZ62-80735]; **p.110** *t* © The Estate of David Gahr/Premium Archive/Getty Images , *b* © ZUMA Press, Inc./Alamy Stock Photo; **p.111** *tl* © Library Of Congress, Prints and Photographic Division [LC-USZ62-5513], *tr* © Patrick Box/Gamma-Rapho/ Getty Images, *bl* © Topham Picturepoint/TopFoto, *br* © ZUMA Press, Inc./Alamy Stock Photo; **p.112** *l* © Paul Wishart/123RF, *r* © Fresnel/Shutterstock; **p.113** *l* © C K Lim/Shutterstock, *r* © PETA; **p.114** *t* © Belizar/Fotolia, *b* © Belizar/Shutterstock; **p.117** *l* © Art Collection 2/Alamy Stock Photo, *r* © AF Fotografie/Alamy Stock Photo; **p.118** © NSPCC 2017. Registered charity England and Wales 216401. Scotland SC037717. Photography by Tom Hull; **p.119** © Volontaire; **p.124** © Michael Jung/Shutterstock; **p.125** *tl* © Richard Gardner/Shutterstock/Rex Features, *tr* © Wellcome Library, London, Creative Commons Attribution only licence CC BY 4.0 http://creativecommons.org/licenses/by/4.0/, *bl* © Photo Researchers/Science History Images/Alamy Stock Photo, *br* © Prisma Archivo/Alamy Stock Photo; **p.126** © Christos Georghiou/Shutterstock.com; **p.127** © Brookm/ Shutterstock; **p.128** *l* © Rockstar Photography/Alamy Stock Photo, *r* © Cultura Creative (RF)/Phil Boorman/Alamy Stock Photo; **p.129** © LARIBOISIERE-APHP-GARO/Phanie/Alamy Stock Photo; **p.131** © Suzi44/Shutterstock; **p.134** ©The National Autistic Society; **p.135** ©The National Autistic Society; **p.144** © Art Collection 2/Alamy Stock Photo; **p.145** *tl* © Topham/PA/ TopFoto, *ml* © National Pictures/TopFoto, *tr* © Interfoto/Personalities/Alamy Stock Photo, *m* © Ria Novosti/TopFoto, *bl* © UPP/ TopFoto, *mb* © Globe Photos/ZUMAPRESS.com/Alamy Stock Photos, *br* © Lisa O›Connor/ZUMA Press, Inc./Alamy Stock Photo; **p.146** *t* © Chris George/Alamy Stock Photo, *b* © World History Archive/TopFoto; **p.150** © www.robot-hugs.com 2013

Text credits

p.11 The article 'Teenage schoolboy cracks Isaac Newton's 300-year-old maths problem', taken from www.thelocal.de, 23 May 2012. Reprinted by permission of The Local Germany; **p.35** The poem 'Translate' by Benjamin Zephaniah. Reprinted with permission of Bloodaxe Books, on behalf of the author www.bloodaxebooks.com; **p.38** The article 'Text speak designed to keep parents in the dark: English language is changing so fast there are words majority do not understand' by Ben Spencer for the *Daily Mail*, 1 May 2015. Reproduced by permission of Solo Syndication; **pp.52–53** An extract from *Touching the Void* by Joe Simpson. © Jo Simpson 1998. Published in the UK by Jonathan Cape. Published as *Essays* by George Orwell with an introduction by Bernard Crick by Penguin Books Ltd (2000), World excl. US ebook rights granted by Penguin Book Ltd. US rights granted by permission of HarperCollins Publishers; **p.65** Amnesty International advert 'How to Give' is taken from http://amnestyinternationalamsterdam.blogspot.co.uk and used by permission of Amnesty International; **p.67** A passage from *Around the World in 80 Days* by Michael Palin. Copyright © Michael Palin 1989, 2008. Reproduced by permission of The Orion Publishing Group, London; **p.71** An extract from *Going Solo* by Roald Dahl. Published by Jonathan Cape Ltd and Penguin Books Ltd © Roald Dahl Nominee Limited. Reprinted with the kind permission of David Higham Associates; **p.76** An extract from 'Marrakech' from *A Collection of Essays* by George Orwell (Copyright © George Orwell, 1939 and renewed 1974 by Sonia Brownell Orwell.) Reprinted by permission of Bill Hamilton as the Literary Executor of the Estate of the Late Sonia Brownell Orwell. Published as *Essays* by George Orwell with an Introduction by Bernard Crick by Penguin Books Ltd (2000), World excl. US ebook rights granted by Penguin Books Ltd. US ebook rights granted by permission of Houghton Mifflin Harcourt Publishing Company. All rights reserved; **p.77** excerpt from *The Great Railway Bazaar* by Paul Theroux. Copyright © Paul Theroux, 1975, 2008, used by permission of The Wylie Agency (UK) Limited; **pp.82–83** An extract from 'Thailand: The Beach revisited', by Michelle Jana Chan, taken from *The Telegraph*, 19 Feb 2010. Reproduced by permission of The Telegraph Media Group Limited; **p.83** An extract from *The Beach* by Alex Garland (1996) published by Penguin Books Ltd and reproduced by permission of Andrew Nurnberg Associates; **pp.86–87** An extract from 'Copenhagen' from *Neither Here Nor There* by Bill Bryson. Copyright © 1991 by Bill Bryson. First published in the UK by Martin Secker & Warburg Ltd and later by Black Swan. UK & World rights granted by permission of The Random House Group Ltd. Published in Canada by Anchor Canada/Doubleday Canada and reproduced with permission of Penguin Random House Canada Limited. US & Philippine rights granted by permission of HarperCollins Publishers; **pp.93–94** Extracts from an article entitled 'Why We Love Traditions, According to Science' by JR Thorpe, taken from www.bustle.com, 23 Dec 2015. Reproduced by permission of Bustle; **p.97** The poem 'Presents from my Aunts in Pakistan' by Moniza Alvi from *Peacock Luggage* by Moniza Alvi and Peter Daniels. Published by Smith/Doorstop Books. Reprinted with permission of Bloodaxe Books, on behalf of the author www.bloodaxebooks.com; **pp.99–105** The short story 'The Lottery' by Shirley Jackson is reprinted by permission of the Shirley Jackson estate; **p.107** Copyright © Amanda Foreman, "Why Footbinding Persisted in China for a Millennium", originally published in Smithsonian Magazine, February 2015, used by permission of The Wylie Agency (UK) Limited; **p.121** A quote from the World Health Organization, 1996. Reproduced with permission; **pp.139–141** An extract from *The Curious Incident of the Dog in the Night-Time* by Mark Haddon copyright © 2003 by Mark Haddon. Published in the UK by Jonathan Cape and UK and World rights granted by permission of The Random House Group Ltd. Published in Canada, USA & the Philippines by Doubleday, an imprint of the Knopf Doubleday Publishing Group, a division of Penguin Random House LLC. All rights reserved.

Visible Thinking – ideas, framework, protocol and thinking routines – from Project Zero at the Harvard Graduate School of Education have been used in many of our activities. You can find out more at: **www.visiblethinkingpz.org**